On
Loyalty

Loyalty is a highly charged and important issue, often evoking strong feelings and actions. What is loyalty? Is loyalty compatible with impartiality? How do we respond to conflicts of loyalties? In a global era, should we be trying to transcend loyalties to particular political communities?

Drawing on a fascinating array of literary and cinematic examples—*The Remains of the Day, No Country for Old Men, The English Patient, The Third Man*, and more—Troy Jollimore expertly unravels the phenomenon of loyalty from a philosophical standpoint. He reflects on the idea that loyalty shapes our very identities, and considers both the benefits and the dangers of loyalty: on the one hand, how excessive loyalty can move us to perform immoral, even evil, actions; one the other, how loyalty can expand our lives and give us a sense of meaning and belonging.

Troy Jollimore is Professor of Philosophy at California State University, Chico, USA. He is the author of *Love's Vision*, and of the National Book Critics Circle Award-winning book of poetry *Tom Thomson in Purgatory*. His essays and book reviews have appeared in *Boston Review, Wilson Quarterly, LA Times, Chicago Tribune*, and elsewhere.

Thinking in Action

Simon Critchley

The New School University, USA

Richard Kearney

Boston College, USA, and University College Dublin, Ireland

Thinking in Action is a major new series that takes philosophy to its public. Each book in the series is written by a major international philosopher or thinker, engages with an important contemporary topic, and is clearly and accessibly written. The series informs and sharpens debate on issues as wide ranging as the Internet, religion, the problem of immigration and refugees, criticism, architecture, and the way we think about science. Punchy, short, and stimulating, **Thinking in Action** is an indispensable starting point for anyone who wants to think seriously about major issues confronting us today.

Praise for the series

". . . allows a space for distinguished thinkers to write about their passions."
The Philosophers' Magazine

". . . deserve high praise."
Boyd Tonkin, *The Independent* (UK)

"This is clearly an important series. I look forward to receiving future volumes."
Frank Kermode, author of *Shakespeare's Language*

". . . both rigorous and accessible."
Humanist News

". . . the series looks superb."
Quentin Skinner

". . . an excellent and beautiful series."
Ben Rogers, author of *A. J. Ayer: A Life*

"Routledge's *Thinking in Action* series is the theory junkie's answer to the eminently pocketable Penguin 60s series."
Mute Magazine (UK)

"Routledge's new series, Thinking in Action, brings philosophers to our aid. . . ."
The Evening Standard (UK)

". . . a welcome series by Routledge."
Bulletin of Science, Technology and Society (Canada)

"Routledge's innovative new 'Thinking in Action' series takes the concept of philosophy a step further."
The Bookwatch

TROY JOLLIMORE

On
Loyalty

Routledge
Taylor & Francis Group

LONDON AND NEW YORK

This edition published 2013
by Routledge
2 Park Square, Milton Park, Abingdon, Oxon, OX14 4RN

Simultaneously published in the USA and Canada
by Routledge
270 Madison Avenue, New York, NY 10016

Routledge is an imprint of the Taylor & Francis Group, an **informa** business

British Library Cataloguing in Publication Data
A catalogue record for this book is available from the British Library

Library of Congress Cataloging in Publication Data
Jollimore, Troy A., 1971-
  On loyalty / Troy Jollimore.
    p. cm. — (Thinking in action)
  Includes bibliographical references and index.
  ISBN 978-0-415-61457-3 (hardback : alk. paper) — ISBN
  978-0-415-78227-2 (pbk. : alk. paper) — ISBN 978-0-203-10763-8 (e-book)
  1. Loyalty.   I. Title.
  BJ1533.L8J65 2012
  179'.9-dc23

                                                                2012023905

HBK ISBN13: 978-0-415-61457-3
PBK ISBN13: 978-0-415-78227-2
EBK ISBN13: 978-0-203-10763-8

Typeset in Joanna MT and Din
by RefineCatch Limited, Bungay, Suffolk

Printed and bound in Great Britain by
TJ International Ltd, Padstow, Cornwall

Contents

Introduction

When Eizaburo Ueno, a professor of agriculture at the University of Tokyo, passed away unexpectedly in May 1925, he left behind a dog, a purebred golden brown *Akita Inu* that he had named Hachi. Hachi had been Professor Ueno's pet for a little over a year, and had fallen into the habit of meeting his train at the Shibuya Station at three o'clock every afternoon. Following the professor's death, Hachi continued to show up at that station just before three every afternoon, until his own death nine years later. The dog—now known as Hachiko—became famous as a symbol of loyalty and dedication throughout Japan. After his death a statue of him was erected in the station where he used to wait. An annual ceremony in Hachiko's honor draws hundreds of dog lovers to the spot. The story has inspired a number of magazine articles and books. 1987 saw the appearance of a Japanese feature film, *The Tale of Hachiko*; in 2009 there was an American film, *Hachi: A Dog's Tale*, starring Richard Gere. In *Hachiko Waits*, a children's book from 2004, we find the following passage:

> From that day on, people from all over Japan came to see
> *Chuken* Hachiko, the famous dog who sat in Shibuya Station
> waiting for his master. Many people who had fallen on hard
> times drew strength from meeting him. "If Hachiko does

not give up hope, we will not give up hope," they said to one another. Many people stroked Hachiko's fur, believing that touching him would bring them good fortune. Those who could gave the Station-Master money so that the *Akita-ken* would not go hungry. Everyone who met Hachiko was moved by his loyalty and devotion.[1]

Stories of loyal dogs are not difficult to find. Indeed, the loyal dog story has become a fairly standard part of the body of tales and urban legends that arises after a catastrophe of any sort. YouTube and other online sites are replete with videos such as "Grave 305: Loyal Dog Sits by Grave of Floods Victim in Brazil" and (following the 2011 tsunami and earthquake that devastated Japan) "Ultimate Loyalty: Japanese Dog Refuses to Leave Injured Friend Behind." A YouTube search for "loyal dog" conducted on 28 May 2011 turned up over 3600 videos with such titles as "Loyal Dog Stays by Deceased Owner's Side" and "Soldier, Loyal Dog Make Final Journey Together." (A search for "loyal husband," by comparison, turned up just over 650 videos.)

But perhaps we are being too quick in applying the word "loyalty" to Hachiko and his kind. Can a dog really be loyal, or possess any virtue in the full-blooded sense? Some people might feel some hesitation saying this, akin to what the philosopher John McDowell expresses when he refers to "the courageous behavior—so called only by courtesy—of a lioness defending her cubs."[2] McDowell's intuition is that while the lioness's behavior resembles courage in some respects, something is lacking, preventing it from amounting to genuine courage. Similarly, we might feel that something in the behavior of Hachiko, or any other dog for that matter, prevents such behavior from amounting to genuine loyalty—despite the fact that such canine behavior is sometimes taken as the very paradigm of loyalty.

The issue is complicated, of course, by the fact that there is much disagreement about animal cognition. Just what is going through the mind of a creature like Hachiko when he shows up at the train station, day after day, seemingly awaiting his master's return? It's hard to say. What we *can* observe is a kind of consistency of behavior over time, and, in particular, a kind of attachment. Hachiko's steadfast attachment to a particular person—his commitment to meeting the train every day, and his apparent refusal to accept that his master is not going to return and to find somebody else to be his companion—is what looks like loyalty to us. But what, then, might be missing from such a case that would explain our hesitation to call this loyalty in the fullest sense?

Perhaps we tend to think of animals as fairly crude machines, so that their behavior is not the result of thought in any genuine sense at all: it is more or less automatic, and not preceded by any sort of deliberation. (This is presumably what McDowell assumes is going on in the lioness case.) Perhaps we do not think of Hachiko as having a genuine choice about how to act. Rather, he just shows up every day like clockwork. Or perhaps he does not have the sort of awareness of time that would inform him that with each day the likelihood of his master's return grows smaller. If every day feels like the first day to Hachiko, then the consistency of his behavior seems less a matter of loyalty than the result of a kind of ignorance.[3]

Another possibility is that Hachiko's "loyalty" fails to be self-reflective in a way that makes it seem not only deficient but a little bit disturbing. After all, the dog's commitment seems to involve no evaluation of the owner—his attachment to Professor Ueno does not in any way express a considered view that Ueno is a good man, worthy of such devotion. And this might remind us of some human attachments, cases in which people stood by or obeyed a spouse, friend, or political leader who did not merit their loyalty.

But even if this is so, should it disqualify Hachiko's behavior as loyalty? Some people think that the virtues, being good character traits, must always lead to good consequences; and if we accept this view then we will indeed find ourselves pushed in the direction of denying that the kind of non-self-reflective commitment displayed by Hachiko could be a true example of loyalty. But this seems to idealize virtue too much: it is surely at least sometimes the case that loyalty is not self-reflective, that sometimes it positively discourages objectivity and self-criticism, and that it therefore sometimes leads to bad behavior and regrettable consequences. We seem to be faced with two alternatives: either accept that the virtues can at least sometimes lead to bad things, or deny that loyalty is a virtue.

THE TWO FACES OF LOYALTY

The common view is that loyalty is a virtue. Indeed, William Bennett devotes a chapter to loyalty in his *Book of Virtues*. "Our loyalties," Bennett writes, "are important signs of the kinds of persons we have chosen to become. They mark a kind of constancy or steadfastness in our attachments . . . Real loyalty endures inconvenience, withstands temptation, and does not cringe under assault. Yet the trust that genuine loyalty tends to generate can pervade our whole lives."[4]

And if loyalty is typically seen as a virtue, its opposing terms—disloyalty, betrayal, treason—are almost universally viewed as moral vices. This is particularly true in the realm of politics, where to allow oneself to be perceived as disloyal is frequently a form of political suicide. One of the guiding thoughts of this book is that genuine loyalty is always "from the inside," in the sense that one can only be fully loyal to a community to which one belongs. The concern with loyalty in the political sphere, then, tends to reflect people's fears and anxieties about being infiltrated, corrupted, and subverted by outside influences. Accusations of disloyalty are nearly always code for "you are not one of us," which helps to explain why overzealous practitioners of dirty politics are inordinately fond of accusing their opponents of that particular "vice." Ann Coulter's *Treason: Liberal Treachery from the Cold War to the War on Terror* represents a recent and particularly vitriolic example. Nor are historical examples hard to find.[5] Jonathan Glover offers the example of Horatio "Horace" Bottomley, a British member of parliament who helped to incite anti-German fervor at the beginning of World War I:

> "I call for a vendetta—a vendetta against every German in Britain—whether 'naturalized' or not . . . You cannot 'naturalize' an unnatural abortion, a hellish freak. But you *can* exterminate him." [Bottomley] urged that naturalized Germans should be made to wear a distinctive badge and not be allowed out after dark. Their children should be excluded from schools. And he further supported this treatment of Germans by encouraging fantasies of them being stripped of protective dignity. After the war, "If by chance you should discover one day in a restaurant you are being served by a German waiter, you will spill the inkpot over his foul head."[6]

The fact that loyalty so easily lends itself to such uses is one of the clearest available reminders that we should not always treat loyalty as a virtue. The fear of outsiders, and the desire to brand as outsiders those among us who express dissent—along with the need for those whose careers depend on popular approval to deal with these public sentiments by proving somehow that they *are* loyal and thus *do* belong—can not only distort and pervert otherwise good intentions but, worse, can allow those who indulge in jingoism to place the stamp of moral goodness on their intolerant and, at times, murderous actions:

> Robert Prager, a German-born coal miner, was accused in April 1918 by a crowd that swelled to 500 people of hoarding explosives outside of St. Louis. Prager, who had tried to enlist in the navy but had been rejected on medical grounds, was stripped, bound with an American flag, dragged barefoot and stumbling through the streets, and lynched as the mob cheered. At the trial of the leaders of the lynch mob, their defense counsel argued that the killing was justifiable "patriotic murder." It took the jury twenty-five minutes to return a not guilty verdict. One jury member shouted out, "Well, I guess nobody can say we aren't loyal now." The *Washington Post* wrote of the trial that "in spite of the excesses such as lynching, it is a healthful and wholesome awakening of the interior of the country."[7]

As such examples suggest, what often turns out to be especially dangerous is the need to demonstrate one's loyalty—to prove to one's fellows that one is a team player, possessed of the proper patriotic sentiments. And what better way to demonstrate the depth of one's commitment than to show that one is willing to commit the most horrible acts of violence? This is particularly true, perhaps, when such acts are committed against people toward whom one would ordinarily bear strong ties of loyalty. "Thou knowest not how sweet is the *amor patriae*," wrote Colucci Salutati in the 14th century. "If such would be expedient for the fatherland's protection or enlargement, it would seem neither burdensome nor a crime to thrust the axe into one's father's head, to crush one's brothers, to deliver from the womb of one's wife the premature child with the sword."[8]

Recent events provide evidence for the power of such sentiments. On 16 March 1968, American soldiers in so-called "Charlie" company murdered—and, in many cases, tortured and raped—hundreds of Vietnamese civilians, mostly women, children, and elderly persons, in the Vietnamese hamlets of My Lai and My Khe. The massacre, now known as the My Lai massacre, eventually became one of the most notorious atrocities committed during the Vietnam War. For years after the event, however, many in the American military and general public downplayed the significance of the event or even praised those who carried it out. The few soldiers who had tried to stop the massacre and protect the innocent victims were denounced by members of the U.S. Congress, received hate mail and death threats from the public, and had mutilated animals placed on their doorsteps. Of the obedient soldiers who had followed their orders and slaughtered scores of defenseless civilians, Staff Sergeant Kenneth Hodges said: "As one of the sergeants who trained Charlie Company, I was very pleased with the way they turned out. They turned out to be very good soldiers. The fact that they were able to go into My Lai and carry out the orders they had been given, I think this is a direct result of the good training they had."[9]

American military personnel continue to place a high value, perhaps excessively high, on loyalty to their country, commanding officers, and fellow soldiers. Concerns about the effect of training that emphasizes these character traits on the ability of soldiers to retain and meaningfully exercise an independent moral conscience did not disappear with the end of the Vietnam conflict. Eric Felten observes that "In 2006, only 37 percent of [U.S. army] troops asked said they 'would report a unit member for the mistreatment of a noncombatant.' And what if someone in your squad killed an innocent noncombatant? In 2007, only 41 percent said they would report it, as opposed to 45 percent the year before."[10]

The rhetoric of loyalty can be used not only to convince people to do harm but also to persuade them to accept being harmed. On the eve of the internment of thousands of Japanese-Americans following the attack on Pearl Harbor, those about to be confined to so-called "War Relocation Camps" received a message from the Japanese-American Citizens League. "You are not being accused of any crime," the message began. "You are being removed only to protect you and because there might be one of you who might be dangerous to the United States. It is your contribution to the war effort. You should be glad to make the sacrifice to prove your loyalty."[11]

Why is it that loyalty can sometimes be so admirable, and at other times so dangerous? Part of the explanation is apparent and indeed obvious: it all depends on who you are loyal to. It is easy and nearly irresistible to praise the loyalty of those who are loyal to us, or to the things that we are loyal to. And it is easy to disapprove of those whose loyalties may conflict with our own, and whose loyalties may therefore make them dangers to us and our interests. Casting our sights wider, we can make judgments about how admirable a certain loyalty is—or isn't—even in cases in which we are not personally involved. The loyalties of those who remained loyal to Hitler throughout World War II, or loyal to Stalin through the purges, were not at all admirable.

Of course, loyalty is not the only virtue that can lead to bad results or be turned to undesirable purposes. A person who serves an evil cause can do so courageously, while an excessively honest person might spoil a child's innocent happiness by telling her there is no Santa Claus. But loyalty, much more than courage or honesty, seems to set us at cross-purposes with one another. If I am loyal to my loved ones then I am prepared to look out for their interests, to some extent, even at the expense of yours. If I am loyal to my loved ones, and you to yours, then at the very least the *possibility* of conflict is inevitable. This is not to say, of course, that anything goes; and if we both observe appropriate moral limits on our behavior then such conflict as might arise will likely be kept within manageable limits. And to say that the possibility of conflict is inevitable is not to say that actual conflict will of necessity occur. Still, loyalty does tend to give us goals that conflict with the goals of others, and so seems by its very nature to set us at odds with one another in a way that most other alleged virtues do not.

We might put the point another way. Most virtues do not seem to be directed toward specific individual people. The kind person is kind to everyone. The honest person is honest to everyone, at least ordinarily. But the loyal person cannot be loyal to everyone; that is incoherent. The virtue of loyalty tells us to be especially virtuous toward some people, and not toward others; and *not*, moreover, because those particular people are especially deserving. How can this be reasonable?

THE BENEFIT OF THE DOUBT

From certain perspectives, then, both the value and rationality of loyalty can be questioned. There are cases, though, in which we are likely to find the value of loyalty hard to deny. Suppose a person is falsely accused of a crime and, as a result, is shunned by most of society; but he has friends or close relatives who refuse to believe the charges and continue to stand by him, even at some cost to themselves. (Real-life examples of such situations are not too hard to find; consider the case of Wen Ho Lee, for instance.) Even if you never actually find yourself in such a situation, knowing that you have people to fall back on if you do can make a substantial difference to your happiness and sense of well-being, and to how you not only evaluate but quite literally understand your life. As Felten asks: "Who would walk the tightrope of life without the net of faithful friends and family?"[12]

There surely is something praiseworthy about the loyalty that is displayed in such cases. As before, though, accounting for the praiseworthiness is not as easy as it may look. Loyalty to a person often tells us to treat that particular individual well, consistently over time; it tells us to be attentive to her, to refuse to speak ill of her, to rise to her defense if she is disparaged or attacked, perhaps even to treat her needs, desires, and interests as if they had an importance that rivaled our own. But again, we can easily understand why we might treat people in such ways; what is potentially mysterious is how our loyalty to somebody can give us an *additional* reason to treat her in such ways, on the hypothesis that she does not *otherwise* deserve it and that the balance of reasons does not *otherwise* favor doing so.

Imagine a case in which someone is falsely accused, but it is not obvious to everyone that the accusation is false; in such a case one's loyalty, or lack thereof, might well make the difference as to whether one presumes the accused innocent, considers him likely guilty, or refrains from making any judgment one way or the other. This is particularly so, perhaps, when the relevant uncertainties are not about the actions that were performed so much as the interpretation of those actions and of what the agent's motives and intentions might have been. If we imagine a continuum of possible responses—from "he is guilty" to "he should have known better" to "I would have done the same" to "he did the right thing"—we can see how a loyal friend will be willing to travel much further along that continuum than a more impartial evaluator would, being willing to give one's friend the benefit of the doubt so long as there remains any doubt at all.

Such willingness can sometimes be justified by the fact that it might let us perceive truths that would otherwise escape us. Giving a friend the benefit of the doubt in this way might let us see how his behavior, in fact, *was* reasonable or even admirable, despite the fact that it initially appeared to us, or would strike an impartial observer, as an error if not a crime.[13] There is also a second kind of justification available here, which is that people, unlike beliefs, are moral patients, so that while it is reasonable and not at all cruel or heartless to evaluate beliefs solely on the basis of the available evidence, evaluating human individuals in this way is another matter altogether. People, that is, *deserve* to be given the benefit of the doubt much of the time; rather than immediately writing them off as bad, it is often much better to try hard to understand why they have chosen to act as they have. In an ideal world we would make this effort on everyone's behalf. In an ideal world, moreover, there would be no deep conflicts between individuals, so we would never be put in the position of having to choose between taking one side or another. But since the world is not ideal, we can only fully make this effort on behalf of some, and sometimes we have to take sides. The group of individuals who consistently receive this empathetic and attentive treatment from you is at least roughly co-extensive with the group of people to whom you are, in a certain sense of the word, loyal.

The positive value of loyalty is often easiest to see and appreciate in cases such as this, which involve the sort of loyalty to individuals that tends to feature in personal relationships such as those of friendship and love. As individuals, we all rely on the loyalty of those who care about us, and we rely on our own loyalty to individuals to give our lives shape and purpose. Moreover, I have argued in an earlier book for a philosophical account of love that takes individual persons to deserve, by dint of their metaphysical nature, certain emotional commitments that express appreciation, caring, and concern.[14] Partly because I have dealt with such relationships at some length in that book, this one tends to focus more on loyalty claims directed toward entities and institutions larger than human beings: countries, nations, and other political communities, as well as businesses and sports teams. This focus, though, is not exclusive, for consideration of personal loyalties is unavoidable, in part because they can sometimes shape, conflict with, or undermine other sorts of loyalties. Moreover, while it may be generally true that loyalties are easier to approve and endorse when directed toward individual persons than when directed toward nations, states, or other larger entities, it will be seen that this is not, in my view, universally true. Indeed, there is no object of loyalty so deserving that loyalty to it is guaranteed to be morally admirable; conversely, while there may be particular objects of loyalty that are so inappropriate or so potentially dangerous that loyalty to them cannot possibly be morally justified, there is no broadly construed type of entity with respect to which this claim can be reliably made.

Loyalty, whatever it is directed toward, always involves an element of risk. Giving the wrong person the benefit of the doubt can mean serving as an apologist for some pretty deplorable behavior. This is part of what accounts for our uncertainty about whether loyalty is a virtue. At times, it calls us to be morally better people than we would otherwise be. On other occasions, it can lead us to be less good than we might otherwise be, to overlook the common humanity that binds us to all human beings and label some people as foreigners or strangers who are unworthy of moral concern. In this book I want to explore these complicated and sometimes contradictory impulses. I do not intend to sugarcoat or whitewash loyalty's moral hazards; indeed, my experience has been that the more I think about it, the more morally hazardous it seems. It is doubtful, moreover, that we will ever be able to render loyalty entirely innocuous. But by illuminating the landscape of loyalty, we might be able to decrease the moral danger that it poses, while at the same time putting ourselves into a better position to be able to appreciate its considerable value.

Loyal Action, Loyal Thought

One

As we saw earlier, William Bennett claims that "our loyalties are important signs of the kinds of persons we have chosen to become." But why stop there? Surely our loyalties are important indications of the kinds of persons we *are*, whether or not we have chosen to become such persons. And surely my loyalties are not only *signs* of the kind of person I am; they in large part *define* the person I am. My loyalties, that is, are important and perhaps fundamental constituents of my identity. That this is so will be one of the recurring themes of this book.

By affecting who we are at a very deep level, our loyalties strongly influence our behavior and the decisions we make. In influencing and shaping our very perceptions of the world, they shape our perceptions of what must be done, of what counts as reasonable behavior, of what sacrifices we are prepared to make, and even of what counts, for us, as a sacrifice. Understanding what loyalty is includes coming to an understanding of the way in which it changes one's ways of thinking, of perceiving, and of being in the world.

LOYALTY, COMMUNITY, SACRIFICE

One of the hallmarks of genuine loyalty is its connection to sacrifice. All true instances of loyalty require sacrifice or, at the very least, a willingness to sacrifice for the good of the

1 | **Loyal Action, Loyal Thought**

person or thing to whom or which one is loyal. Depending on the circumstances, one might be called on to give up material goods or financial interests, to perform inconvenient or odious tasks, to risk one's safety if not one's very life, and to perform acts one would ordinarily regard as positively immoral.

Let's begin with so-called "brand loyalty." Consider a person who has a brand of, say, toothpaste that he always buys, simply because he thinks it the best toothpaste on the market. Let us suppose that if the supermarket he usually frequents were to stop carrying it, he would switch to a nearby supermarket that does carry it. In a sense, this person displays loyalty. But let us also suppose that if another company were to begin selling, at a lower price, a product that he was convinced was equally good, he would buy their product instead. Or suppose that he would even settle for a slightly inferior product if it were substantially cheaper. If this is so then it does not appear that he is genuinely loyal to the brand at all: his commitment is too weak, too shallow, and too thoroughly self-interested.

Of course, there may be reasons why he might be reluctant to switch to another brand. It might be that, in fact, there is, on the market, a product just as good as his brand, and for the same price. But he does not know this; and even if someone alerts him to the fact that it might be so, he might not be inclined to investigate. He is already happy enough with the brand he currently uses, and there are costs, and risks, to that kind of survey. We can expect, then, a certain degree of consistent behavior on his part. This sort of inertia could be considered a kind of loyalty; but again, as far as commitments go, it is shallow indeed, since we are imagining that if he *knew* that another kind of toothpaste would be slightly more satisfying, not only immediately but in the long term, he would not hesitate to make the switch.

Suppose, on the other hand, that he would hesitate to switch to another brand even if he were convinced that the alternative was, in fact, a better deal for him: if, that is, it were cheaper but did an equally good job, or it cost the same but did a better job, or it were equally cheap and equally good but more convenient to obtain, etc. At this point it becomes reasonable to see the consistent behavior he exhibits as a kind of loyalty. Up to this point there is no real attachment to the brand itself, only an intelligible and reasonable policy of conservatism about changing one's habits. And what is interesting is that the point where it first seems appropriate to call his behavior a form of loyalty is precisely the point at which it begins to display what looks, at least from the perspective of self-interest, like an irrational element. For if he knows that another brand of toothpaste would be more satisfying in the long run—or would be equally satisfying in itself, and is available for a lower price—then why would he hesitate?

There are possible answers to this question. Imagine, for instance, that he is friends with the person who runs the Acme Toothpaste Company, and values the fact that he supports his friends through his dedication to their products. In this situation talk of loyalty seems quite appropriate. Of course, this is an unusual and unlikely situation, at least with respect to toothpaste. But a person who frequents a certain restaurant, bar, or independent bookstore might get to know the owners and the establishment's clientele, and it would not be unnatural for such a person to end up feeling a certain loyalty to these people and to that particular business. Such a person would, presumably, be willing to undergo certain sacrifices (paying slightly higher prices for books than he would online or at the local corporate chain bookstore, for instance). Similarly, someone who has spent his entire life working for General Motors, for instance—or whose father did so—might insist on buying cars made by GM, and might be willing to continue doing so even if he came to believe that some competitor's cars were more reliable, or better made, or in some other way a superior value for the money.

The situation is complicated, though, because to say that loyalty must transcend the claims of "narrow self-interest" is not to say that the loyal person will necessarily perceive the demands her loyalties make as being *opposed* to her self-interest. People tend to identify with the objects of their loyalties, particularly where those objects are communities of whom they are members. They tend, that is, to see the interests of those communities as being merged to a considerable extent with their own interests. What would be considered a sacrifice from the perspective of narrow self-interest, then, might not feel like one at all to the person making it. Consider a much more dramatic sort of case, that of going to war. If you see your country as, literally, an extension of yourself—so that an injury done to it is also, automatically, an injury done to you—then risking your life in defense of your country will strike you not as a sacrifice, but as a form of self-defense.

Some thought of this sort is often required to motivate people to kill and die in war. Most people who receive ordinary upbringings are quite averse to violence; after all, pointing a gun at someone else and pulling the trigger is not something most people would ordinarily consider, and it is not, for most, something that is easy to do. The strategy here is not only to get individuals to see loyal actions, even those that threaten their well-being or very lives, as involving a kind of self-interest—though this is an important element of it—but also to tie this expanded notion of identity to questions of significance, meaning, and worth. Living loyally, and making the sacrifices demanded by loyalty, come to be seen as practices that enrich a person's existence; indeed, they must come to be perceived in this way if appeals to the rhetoric of loyalty are to be effective, particularly in cases where acting as loyalty demands means putting one's life on the line, or performing actions that would otherwise strike one as morally repellent.

Thus, while it is common to think of obligations arising from self-interest as being entirely separate from obligations arising from the interests and needs of other individuals, or of the community at large, one of the functions of loyalty seems to be to merge these two sorts of obligation, at least in the mind of the loyal person. This is in line with a way of thinking about the virtues that seems to originate with the ancient Greek philosophers, Aristotle in particular. We moderns, when we think about virtues at all, tend to choose one of two conceptual paths: we conceive of the virtues either as character traits whose possession tends to benefit the individual who possesses them, or as character traits whose possession is good for the community in general. But if we are influenced by a certain line of Aristotelian thought, we might see little if any difference between these two conceptions, holding that the properly functioning human being is the one who functions best in her community, and that it is those individuals who will be happiest and best off.

From the standpoint of a loyal citizen of this sort, this will seem to be true, for the loyal citizen already conceives of her community's good as being wrapped up inextricably with her own. Indeed, she probably sees her very identity as being inextricably wrapped up with that of her community, in the sense that she is who she is because of that community, and would not be the same person without it. The flourishing of her community is part of her flourishing, and the survival of her community is part of her survival—a fact that can help explain why, in times of war or other emergency, patriots are willing to risk their very lives to protect the homeland. Nationalism, writes Yael Tamir, has the ability to:

> . . . transform the self-image of individuals by portraying their personal welfare as closely tied to the existence and prosperity of their national community . . . [This transformation] imports special significance to even the most mundane actions and endows individual lives with meaning. It is in this sense that nationalism bestows extra merit on social, cultural, or political acts and provides individuals with additional channels for self-fulfillment that make their lives more rewarding.[1]

Maurizio Viroli imputes a similar view to Machiavelli: "The virtuous citizens whom Machiavelli extols in the *Discourses* serve the common good—the liberty and the law of each city— because they are aware that the common good is the same as the individual interest of each."[2] And Morton Grodzins argues that loyalties are "given in return for gratifications received. They organize the life of the individual, reducing the area of uncertainty and anxiety . . . One is loyal to the groups that provide gratifications because what serves the group serves the self; what threatens the group threatens the self. *There is no self outside group activity.*"[3]

In the real world, of course, things are never quite this clean. It is never literally true, that is, that the common good is exactly identical with anybody's individual good, that "there is no self outside group activity." There always is;

and the demands of the self will inevitably rub up against the constrictions of any sort of group activity one might find oneself involved in. (Moreover there is something disturbingly totalitarian about the desire that such conflict *not* exist.) Still, while the two will never entirely merge, there may often be a considerable degree of overlap, and it is certainly plausible to think that part of being loyal to a community is seeing one's membership in that community, and perhaps one's loyalty itself, as important constituents of one's very identity—a kind of thought that will tend strongly to suggest that one's own good and the good of one's community are, after all, closely tied together.

LOYALTY AND THE EXPANSION OF SELF

Loyalty can thus give one a sense of meaning and purpose, a sense that one's good, and one's fate, are wrapped up with something larger than oneself. Even so small a community as that involved in a friendship or romantic relationship involves an enlargement of one's world and expansion of one's sense of self. On a larger scale, the triumphs and achievements of one's society may be felt to compensate for limits on, or inadequacies in, one's life as an individual. The psychologist Ernest Partridge suggests that human psychology contains a fundamental need to achieve "self transcendence" by connecting one's own projects and strivings with those of other persons, and that human beings who fail to do this will be alienated, in so far as they will "lack significant, fundamental and widespread capacities and features of human moral and social experience."[4]

Of course, overcoming alienation and achieving self-transcendence by identifying one's community's good with one's own can be threatening, since attaching your good to the good of your community opens you up to potential new forms of harm. If your community is destroyed or badly harmed, and you are attached to it through your loyalty, then you are harmed too. By the same token, though, such attachments also open you up to types of good that are not only distinct from, but in some cases larger than, the goods that an individual can experience for herself. Think, for instance, of the way in which Red Sox fans celebrated when "their" team won the World Series in 2004. Whatever one may think of the tendency of a fan to feel that the achievements of his team—a group of individuals whom he has probably never even met, and who are not aware of his existence—are nevertheless his achievements, there is no doubt that this feeling is frequently both sincere and powerful. The kind of imaginative identification that can take place between a fan and the athletes he admires is brilliantly captured in this passage from Frederick Exley's novel *A Fan's Notes*:

Already that fall I had drawn parallels between [Frank] Gifford's life and mine, our having been at USC together, our having come East almost simultaneously, and the unquestionable fact that we both desired fame, perhaps he even more than I, for he had already eaten, in a limited way, of that Bitch at school. Throughout that long autumn, throughout those long, lovely afternoons, there was only one number for me, 16, and I cheered frantically for it, pounding my Brooklyn buddies on the back, and screaming, "Atta boy, Frank! Atta way, you bastard!" I caught passes with him, and threw blocks with him, and groaningly sucked in my breath as he was being viciously tackled. Watching him rise after such a tackle, I piddled back to the huddle with him, my head cranked back at the recent executor of the tackle, my voice warning, "Next time, you bastard—" . . . I cheered for

him with such inordinate enthusiasm, my yearning became
so involved with his desire to escape life's bleak anonymity,
that after a time he became my alter ego, that part of me
which had its being in the competitive world of men; I came,
as incredible as it seems to me now, to believe that I was,
in some magical way, an actual instrument of his success.
Each time I heard the roar of the crowd, it roared in my ears
as much for me as him . . . .[5]

The identifications here proceed on multiple levels. By imaginatively merging his identity with that of his favorite player, the fan also merges his identity with the team, of which that player is a member; and this makes their successes and failures his own in what at least feels like a literal sense. Now he has new things to hope for and fear, new events around which to structure his life, and new goals—and if they are goals he himself cannot actually make much of a contribution toward fulfilling, his imaginative identification may help him to forget that fact by leading him to believe that he is, "in some magical way, an actual instrument of [the team]'s success." Besides, fans do make *some* contribution, however small. They buy tickets, they show up and cheer, and they encourage others to do the same. (And many fans would at least be willing to do more: a recent poll of English soccer fans found that 12 percent of them would be willing to go without sex for a year if doing so meant that England would win the World Cup.)

All of this helps make sense of behaviors such as buying and wearing team jerseys, baseball caps, and other types of athletic insignia. Such acts assist in the imaginative identification with the team at large or with particular players, while also allowing one to be identified by one's fellow loyalists, displaying one's allegiances and helping to clarify the loyalty-based communities of which one is a member. Larger entities than sports teams—nations, for instance—also make use of the human tendency to find meaning in activities that attach the self to a larger community or tribe, and that context, too, has its symbols—wearing a flag pin, installing an actual flag in one's front yard, standing up and singing one's national anthem—that are used to display the allegiances that exist on those levels.

The potency of such symbols has not escaped the notice of advertisers and public relations experts. A corporation might literally put a face on their product, either the face of someone actually connected with the company (Ben and Jerry's ice cream, Newman's Own salad dressing) or of a fictional character (Aunt Jemima, Betty Crocker), in order to help customers identify with them, and so behave not just as customers but, in a sense, as fans. In other more subtle ways, too, corporations encourage their potential customers to think that by buying their product they will become part of a community and adopt a sort of desirable identity. Owning a high-end sports car—say, a Porsche—may be perceived as desirable not only because the car as object is in itself desirable, but because joining the ranks of Porsche-owners is seen as a good thing. One does not just want to own the Porsche; rather, one wants to be the person who owns the Porsche—and thus to be the person who belongs, or at any rate is seen as belonging, among all the other Porsche-owners.

HOPES, BELIEFS, PERCEPTIONS

In addition to requiring a willingness to sacrifice, loyalty seems to require that a person have certain hopes, beliefs, and desires. Along with this, it may also require not only that a person *not* have certain hopes or desires, but also that she not even consider or entertain certain thoughts.

Patriotism, for instance, may seem to require not only that one is prepared to defend one's country, but also that one have certain feelings, and perhaps certain thoughts, about it. There is a patriotic sentiment, a kind of warm attachment and fondness, that a patriot is expected to feel with respect to her country. We must be careful, though, not to define such sentiments too narrowly, or be too restrictive in our accounts of when they ought to be felt. Consider an American protester who, during the Vietnam War, refuses to salute the flag or to rise for the pledge of allegiance. Her belief is that the republic has been corrupted and is no longer run according to its original principles—the principles that the flag and the pledge are in some sense meant to stand for. Such a person might feel no warm sentiment of attachment to her country as the pledge is recited all about her; she might instead feel disappointment and anger at what she regards as the betrayal of her country's ideals. She might, for all that, be genuinely loyal to her country, and in a very real sense a patriot. Indeed, her attachment to her country's ideals, and her rage at their betrayal, are evidence in favor of this claim.

The question of just what we should feel, then, is complicated. The question of what we should *think* is perhaps even more so. It might seem plausible to think that a true patriot should believe that his country is especially worthy and admirable; some would even say that a genuine patriot believes his country to be the best country on Earth. Clearly some people, including many proponents of patriotism, understand the concept in this way. Others have claimed, though, that loyalty does not require one to believe that the object of one's loyalty is objectively valuable. One might hold, for instance, that anyone who is a citizen of *any* country owes a certain amount of patriotic devotion to his country, regardless of what that country is like. Such a view holds that what matters, and what grounds my patriotism, is not that my county is objectively the best, but that my country is *mine*.

Similarly, it is commonly thought that there are special attachments and obligations that connect parents and children and that do not reflect any alleged claim about the worth of the individuals in question. Harry Frankfurt claims that it is not the fact that my children are especially valuable that makes me see them as special; rather, it is the fact that I see them as special that makes them especially valuable *to me*.[6] Or consider the example of sports. One can, it seems, be a fan of a team without believing that they will win or even that they are good enough to win. Think, for instance, of the very loyal fans of the Chicago Cubs, many of whom would be the first to admit that the objects of their affection are not, in fact, very good at playing baseball. If the belief that one's team is likely to win were a requirement of fan loyalty, teams such as the Cubs would have very few fans, and only epistemically irrational ones.[7]

Perhaps, it will be suggested, what patriotism and other forms of loyalty involve is often not so much *beliefs* as *hopes*. I do not have to think that my country is, in fact, the best on Earth, but as a patriot I must hope that its people continue to prosper, and that it does not suffer a total military defeat or other humiliation that would threaten its standing in the world and perhaps even its historical continuity. And if I am the sort of patriot described above (the kind who believes that her country is currently failing to live up to the ideals that once made it worthy), then I must also hope that it somehow overcomes these difficulties and finds its way back to those ideals.

At this point, though, we may find ourselves thinking once more that there are certain beliefs that must be involved. For to hope that one's country prospers and lives up to its ideals commits one to thinking both that it is good enough to be at least potentially capable of rediscovering those ideals, and good enough—in its future, more ideal state if not in its degraded current state—to deserve to prosper. (And one must also believe, of course, that the ideals are worth living up to.) Similarly, Cubs fans may not think that their team is good enough at baseball to win; but if they want them to win then there must be some sense, possibly a moral or quasi-moral sense, in which they feel that the team deserves to win— or, perhaps better, that they deserve to improve to the point where they win. (An intriguing possibility here is that the deservingness might not be possessed so much by the *players* as by the *fans*, that it is the fans' longstanding dedication in the face of adversity that makes *them* worthy of the Cubs' getting better and coming to win.)

Even on the Frankfurtian view, having a special attachment to someone involves seeing her as special. One must see her as having some sort of real value, a value which is, perhaps, difficult for others to see and appreciate. Thus, to say that loyalty need not involve evaluative beliefs in the most straightforward manner—which is just to say that one can be loyal to one's country, one's lover, or one's team without thinking that that country, person, or team is worthier by objective standards than any other potential object of loyalty—is not to say that loyalty is just a brute emotional or volitional commitment that does not involve beliefs, or even evaluative beliefs, of any sort. Some fairly complex network of beliefs is required, not only to make sense of a given case of loyalty, but to make it the case that that particular attachment or commitment counts as an instance of loyalty at all.[8] And the fact that the network of beliefs can take many different forms (some U.S. patriots believe their country literally is the best on Earth, others that it is a flawed country that aspires to greatness or merely to decency) should not obscure the fact that beliefs are nevertheless required, or lead us to conclude, erroneously, that loyalty is just a matter of brute feeling.

This raises issues of perception and bias, since loyalty typically renders a person more prone to forming positive beliefs about her loyalty object. Although it is possible to be a patriot without believing that one's country is objectively the best in the world, patriots will nonetheless tend to, and are perhaps required to, seek out, appreciate, and promote or defend those things that do make it valuable. They must be especially open and receptive to its value, and must feel especially protective of that value. Similarly, as noted earlier, loyalty to an individual person often involves giving him the benefit of the doubt, in the sense that one continues not to be convinced of that person's guilt or blameworthiness even past the point where the evidence would be regarded by an impartial observer as reasonably convincing. This is not simply an intellectual decision or stance—as if you were to see the person in question in essentially the same light as everyone else, but register an internal hesitation or mental reservation. ("Yes, surely she's guilty but I'm not going to say so; after all, she's my friend.") Rather, one will actually *see* the person differently, and will not *feel* her to be guilty or flawed—at least up to the point where the evidence becomes so clearly convincing that the conclusion one has been resisting is undeniable.

Loyalty, in its fullest forms, thus alters both the way one sees the world and the way one feels about it. We should understand this as literally as possible, for the world really does look different to the loyal person, much as it does to the person who is in love. Moreover, the influence of loyalty on one's perceptions is not, as it were, an additional element that is somehow added on *after* the act of perceiving—as if one's initial, more objective perceptions occurred but were then covered with a veneer of generous or charitable interpretation. There is no initial unvarnished view; the tendency to view charitably is present from the very first moment of perception. Of course, one might find oneself in situations in which one's loyalty to another is strained, and in which one has difficulty *not* seeing that person more objectively or dispassionately. In such situations one might need to exert a certain effort to feel, or be, loving or loyal; loyalty will then manifest itself more as an external obligation than as an element of one's own character. But loyalty, at least when wholehearted and unstrained, does not ordinarily manifest itself in this way. Rather, one's loyalty is simply present, conditioning one's perceptions in a manner so deep and pervasive that one will not typically be directly aware of its presence, or of its effects. This is part of what makes loyalty so powerful—and, in some contexts, part of what can make it so dangerous.

THE PERCEPTION OF SACRIFICE

Empirical support for this claim is available, and can come from surprising places. Let us return to the connection between loyalty and sacrifice, and in particular to the toothpaste example. As long as the toothpaste buyer was merely doing what was in his self-interest, I suggested, we would not be inclined to look on his commitment as a genuine case of loyalty. The clearest crossing of that threshold happens when he reaches the point of being willing to do things that are costly to himself in order to benefit the object of his commitment.

That seems right as far as it goes; but as we have already observed, there are complications. One is that a loyal person might see her own interests as being merged with those of the object of her commitment, so that what would otherwise count as a sacrifice ceases to be one. Another possibility is that loyalty might shape our perceptions in such a way that we *believe* that we are acting in our self-interest, when in fact we are actually making sacrifices of which we are not aware.

In a recent study conducted at Baylor University, subjects were given two types of soft drink, Coke and Pepsi, in unmarked cups.[9] Their responses were monitored using an fMRI machine, to see which drink they enjoyed more. Then the subjects were told which types of soft drink they had just consumed. Some of these subjects were loyal Coke-drinkers—people who had drunk Coke all their lives, and who claimed to prefer it to Pepsi. And some of these loyal Coke-drinkers, when presented with the two drinks in unmarked cups, clearly preferred the Pepsi. Let's call these people Coke-Loyalists-Albeit-Pepsi-Preferrers, or CLAPPs for short.

Now here is the interesting part. When a CLAPP was told that the drink in the second cup—the one that he had enjoyed more, according to the brain scan—was Pepsi, two things typically happened. First, the subject reported (falsely, according to the brain scan) that he had actually preferred the drink in the first cup, the Coke, to that in the second cup, the Pepsi. Second, a further brain scan revealed that the brain's pleasure apparatus was actually altered so that the pleasure caused by the Pepsi was now suppressed. The Coke loyalists were not lying, then, in stating their preferences; rather, they genuinely believed that they had preferred the Coke to the Pepsi because they literally do not experience the same thing when they drink Coke that they know is Coke as they do when they drink Coke without knowing what brand it is.

So the situation is, indeed, quite complicated. Suppose a Coke loyalist is willing to suffer some inconvenience, or pay more, to obtain Coke, which he thinks he prefers to Pepsi. And suppose that this person is, in fact, a CLAPP—that is, if he did not know which he was drinking, he would prefer Pepsi to Coke. Such a person does not see himself as making a sacrifice in undergoing a certain amount of inconvenience to obtain Coke. He thinks that he is acting self-interestedly. The truth of the matter is, though, that he would be happier if he simply bought Pepsi, which is easier to obtain, and which actually tastes better to him—or which would taste better to him, if he did not know the name on the label!

It seems reasonable to consider this person as displaying a type of loyalty, despite the fact that he takes himself to be purely self-interested. He is, after all, committed to Coke-drinking even at some cost to himself, even if he does not know this about himself. Many real-world loyalties, we might suspect, work in just this way. Of course, in many cases people might not take themselves to be purely self-interested; rather, they might believe themselves to be willing to make some sacrifices for the sake of what they are loyal to. But they might not realize just how much sacrifice they are making or willing to make, because they might not realize that their very perceptions are themselves biased by their beliefs about the things to which they are committed.

Consider, for instance, a woman who chooses to remain married to a man who abuses her physically and emotionally.

Those around her might think, entirely reasonably and entirely correctly, that she would be better off without him. But this might not be so apparent to her. After all, she sees their lives as inextricably intertwined, and she might well have come to believe that left to stand on her own feet she would not flourish, or even survive. The point is not that she is not aware that there are costs to her remaining in the marriage. As a sufferer of abuse, she certainly knows that there are. Still, she underestimates those costs, while at the same time overestimating the costs that leaving would entail. And these mis-estimations will not manifest themselves simply as entries in a rational ledger, as it were; rather, like the mis-tastings of the subjects of the Baylor study (but in a considerably more serious way), they will influence the very way in which she experiences what happens in her life.

This is important for understanding the way our loyalties function in our decision-making.

The Coke–Pepsi case shows how loyalty can alter one's perceptions, literally changing the way a soft drink tastes to a given individual. A perceptual experience is partly cognitive in so far as it involves a kind of thought. Part of experiencing something as delicious is the belief that the thing being experienced tastes delicious. And while in the simplest cases the belief is formed as a result of the pure experience—we taste something, find that it tastes delicious, and so believe that it is delicious—this sort of case illustrates that the causal influence can run in the other direction as well.

Loyalty can also influence other, more intellectual thoughts. When you leap into the fray to defend your friend against malicious gossip, you are not doing this simply as a matter of obligation—as if you were saying to yourself: "What they are saying about my friend is most likely true, but as her friend it is my obligation to deny it."[10] Rather, if you are genuinely loyal you will tend not to believe the gossip. Indeed, you will be much less likely to believe that gossip than you would be if it were directed toward someone about whom you had neutral feelings—even if you had as much evidence for believing it in the one case as in the other. Thus friendship and other relationships involving loyalty display what philosophers have called *epistemic partiality*. "Epistemic" means we are dealing with questions of belief, knowledge, and justification, so to exhibit epistemic partiality is to be inclined in a certain direction with respect to the way in which you form, adopt, and reject beliefs. A friend is epistemically partial in that she is more likely to make and maintain positive judgments about her friends, and less likely to make and maintain negative beliefs about them, for reasons that are not based on the evidence that she possesses.

As Simon Keller has written: "when good friends form beliefs about each other, they sometimes respond to considerations that have to do with the needs and interests of their friends, not with aiming at the truth, and. . . this is part of what makes them good friends."[11] Similarly, Sarah Stroud has argued that when we are making judgments about a friend's behavior, "we tend to devote more energy to defeating or minimizing the impact of unfavorable data than we otherwise would . . . at the end of the day we are simply less likely to conclude that our friend acted disreputably, or that he is a bad person, than we would in the case of a nonfriend."[12]

As we have already acknowledged, there are limits to this. David Kaczynski, the brother of Ted Kaczynski, was probably reluctant at first to believe that his brother could be the infamous "Unabomber" who had been terrorizing the U.S.

with letter-bombs sent through the mail. Eventually, though, his suspicions overwhelmed whatever loyalty he felt to his brother, and he contacted the FBI. Some might hold that David Kaczynski acted wrongly. It is possible, after all, to hold a theory of family obligation according to which it could *never* be right to report a close relative to the legal authorities, no matter what that person might have done. More of us, I suspect, hold a different view, which is that the discovery that a close relative, or indeed anyone to whom one has been deeply loyal, has committed a serious crime is a true dilemma, a situation in which one cannot be happy about or comfortable with any of the options that one might select. (We will return to this issue of dilemmas and conflicts of loyalty in Chapter Two.) But whatever the limits might be, it seems clear that one of the pressures exerted by a commitment that involves loyalty pushes us to see the object of that commitment in a positive light—which not only involves certain positive thoughts that one will be inclined to direct toward them, but also, and sometimes more significantly, certain thoughts that one will be under very real and considerable pressure *not* to think.

LOYALTY VERSUS REFLECTION

The most difficult thing, when confronted with evidence that a loved one has done a terrible thing, might simply be getting oneself to believe it. The first impulse is nearly always to reject the idea that one's brother is the Unabomber, that one's spouse has committed murder, that one's son or daughter is selling heroin to children. The thought that a person one loves might be engaged in awful behavior is a difficult one to stomach, and the belief in that person's innocence might persist in the face of a mountain of evidence, well past the point when one would have given up on someone to whom one was not attached. What's more, one might fail to notice that a certain bit of evidence *is* evidence. If we aren't positively looking for indications of trouble (and with respect to those we love and are loyal to, we frequently aren't), what hindsight might eventually identify as fairly obvious problem signs might simply escape one's notice.

Among other things, then, epistemic partiality involves the fact that there are thoughts that will simply not occur to the genuinely loyal person—or, if they do, will occur only with the greatest difficulty, well after they would have occurred to someone who was not loyal. Most parents, even those who are sometimes frustrated and displeased with their children's behavior, will find it difficult to believe that one of their children has committed an extremely serious crime; indeed, even in the face of very strong evidence, some parents will continue to insist: "But my son couldn't *possibly* have done *that*." Similarly, a loving husband does not frequently pause to wonder whether his wife is worthy of his love. He finds it difficult to imagine that she might not be worthy, or that she might be seriously deficient in any respect, just as some parents find it difficult to imagine that their own children might be poorly behaved, or that they might be no cuter, no more intelligent, or no more charming than the average child.

This is a point about thinking and believing. But there is a similar point to be made in the practical realm, with respect to practical options and decisions. Our behavior is shaped not only by what we think, but by what we do not think. When you perform an action, you often do so after considering alternatives; but it is impossible to consider every alternative, or even to come close. Suppose you have a certain goal: say, that you wake up in the morning craving chocolate chip muffins, and decide that you want to satisfy this craving somehow. There are perhaps two main alternatives that you will consider: go to the market and buy muffins, or stay home and bake muffins. But these are far from the only possibilities. There are possibilities that you will not bother even to consider because they are so unlikely to work, such as praying for a muffin, or going to the closet in case the muffin elves have visited during the night, or opening your front door and yelling: "Somebody get me a muffin!" And there are an infinite number of alternatives that seem entirely irrelevant to your desire for a muffin: going bowling, washing your face, reading a philosophy book, and so forth. The point is that you do not need to stop to consider each of these alternatives to decide that it is irrelevant or unlikely to work. Indeed, if we did that we would never reach a practical decision because there are literally an infinite number of possible actions.

In addition to those actions that are not considered because they are irrelevant, there are also possibilities that are ruled out in advance for moral reasons. Rather than going to the market and buying muffins, you could go to the market and steal muffins, and kill the baker or anyone else who got in your way. Again, you do not need to deliberate in order to decide that this is a bad plan; rather, you know that without even thinking about it, and the thought of doing this would not even cross your mind.

Everybody's thoughts are shaped in ways like this. But when a person is loyal to someone, her thoughts are shaped in similar but more specific ways, because there are things that she *would* consider (though perhaps not do) with respect to strangers that she would *not* consider doing with respect to the object of her loyalty—and vice versa. If I am on my way to teach a class and I see someone who seems upset, I might note the fact without considering whether I should stop to get involved. After all, I don't want to be late for class—I have an obligation to my students—and I might not want to get involved in affairs that are not mine. If it were a friend of mine, though, I would, of course, stop and try to help—students be damned! Indeed, I would not even consider whether I should stop for a friend who was clearly upset. The thought of just walking on by would quite literally not occur to me, and in the midst of my concern for my friend I would very likely forget all about the conflicting commitments that had seemed, the very moment before, so serious and pressing.

The philosopher John McDowell refers to this phenomenon, in its connection with moral behavior, as *silencing*. An ideally virtuous person, McDowell writes, is simply not tempted to do the morally wrong thing in the sense that the wrong thing simply does not present itself to her as an option. Either it will not occur to her at all or, if it does, it will not attract her—that is, she will not feel the motivational tug or pull that would constitute temptation. The reason for doing the right thing does not overpower competing reasons so much as it undermines them, robbing them of any motivational force they might have, so that such an agent sees "the relevant reasons for acting, on occasions when they co-exist with considerations that on their own would be reasons for acting otherwise, as, not overriding, but silencing those other considerations—as bringing it about that, in the circumstances, they are not reasons at all."[13]

So there are things that a loyal person would not stop to consider, in the sense that they simply would not occur to her. And even if they did occur to her—the mind, after all, is an unruly place—many of these would be things that a loyal person would not only not be tempted to do, they would be things she could not seriously consider doing, and perhaps could not bring herself to do even if she managed to consider them. At the end of the movie *Brazil* (Terry Gilliam, 1984), the film's protagonist, Sam Lowry, is arrested by the oppressive regime he lives under and brought to be interrogated by the torturer, Jack Lint. It happens that Sam and Jack are friends—and, indeed, Jack is quite put out by being in such an awkward position. ("How could you do this to me?" he whines at his victim.) Jack nevertheless decides to go ahead and torture Sam. If nothing else, this decision, and his willingness to carry it through, decisively establishes that the relationship that holds between Sam and Jack is not one of genuine friendship. Torturing a friend ought to be literally unthinkable, in the sense of being something that one could not seriously consider doing.

One might plausibly hold, of course, that torturing *anyone* should be unthinkable. But even if we were all in agreement on this, we could still say that torturing a friend ought to be, so to speak, *even more* unthinkable. Moreover, there are other cases where many people would say that actions that are thinkable and perhaps even justifiable with respect to strangers would be unthinkable with respect to friends. Each of us lives with the awareness that each year millions of people die of starvation or easily preventable diseases, and that we could save some of these lives by donating more of our ample income to charity. Allowing these people to die is not only thinkable, but an actual choice we make. Allowing a friend or close family member to die in this way, on the other hand, when a small amount of money would prevent this from happening, would be unthinkable.

This is one of the many contexts, then, in which loyalty oscillates between being a virtue and being a vice. It can be a spur to moral action by rendering certain moral failures—failures of compassion or of generosity, for instance—to be unthinkable. But it can also silence the demands of many of those who are suffering or are in peril, and blind us to their predicaments, thus encouraging us to exclude those beyond our ken from the realm of moral concern.

Moreover, the very fact that the pressures placed on belief by loyalty are not intrinsically connected with truth raises grave concerns, as one of the effects of loyalty is often to silence doubt, to discourage criticism. Being loyal, it is sometimes thought, is incompatible with taking a critical stance—a thought that is interestingly articulated by Mr. Stevens, the butler who serves as the main character of Kazuo Ishiguro's novel *The Remains of the Day*, when he speaks disparagingly of:

> . . . that strand of opinion in the profession which suggested that any butler with serious aspirations should make it his business to be forever reappraising his employer—scrutinizing the latter's motives, analyzing the implications of his views. Only in this way, so the argument ran, could one be sure one's skills were being employed to a desirable end. Although one sympathizes to some extent with the idealism contained in such an argument, there can be little doubt that it is the result, like Mr. Smith's sentiments tonight, of misguided thinking. One need only look at the butlers who attempted to put such an approach into practice, and one will see that their careers—and in some cases they were highly promising careers—came to nothing as a direct consequence. I personally knew at least two professionals, both of some ability, who went from one employer to the next, forever dissatisfied, never settling anywhere, until they drifted from view altogether. That this should happen is not in the least surprising. For it is, in practice, simply

not possible to adopt such a critical attitude towards an
employer and at the same time provide good service . . .
a butler who is forever attempting to formulate his own
"strong opinions" on his employer's affairs is bound to lack
one quality essential in all good professionals: namely,
loyalty . . . if a butler is to be of any worth to anything or
anybody in life, there must surely come a time when he
ceases his searching; a time when he must say to himself:
"This employer embodies all that I find noble and admirable.
I will hereafter devote myself to serving him." This is loyalty
intelligently bestowed.[14]

Although Stevens does not quite explicitly acknowledge it, he
is not unaware of the deep and somewhat ironic tension in
his view. The fact that one's employer "embodies all that I find
noble and admirable" is supposed to inspire a commitment to
overlook those occasions on which the employer's behavior is
neither noble nor admirable: as when Mr. Stevens's employer,
Lord Darlington, is convinced by his National Socialist friends
to dismiss two of his maids who happen to be Jews. Ever
the loyal servant, Stevens does not protest Lord Darlington's
decision. Miss Kenton, the maids' immediate supervisor, *does*
protest, and Mr. Stevens's attempt to justify his behavior to her
is instructive:

"Miss Kenton, I am surprised to find you reacting in
this manner. Surely I don't have to remind you that our
professional duty is not to our own foibles and sentiments,
but to the wishes of our employer . . . let me suggest to you
that you are hardly well placed to be passing judgments of
such a high and mighty nature. The fact is, the world of today
is a very complicated and treacherous place. There are many
things you and I are simply not in a position to understand

concerning, say, the nature of Jewry. Whereas his lordship, I might venture, is somewhat better placed to judge what is for the best."[15]

Perhaps Stevens is right in thinking that a good servant must refrain from criticism or independent judgment. But if so, then the proper conclusion to draw is probably that the role of servant is not one that a human individual ought to be willing to accept, for it involves a kind of servility that seems incompatible with a human being's respect for himself. By the end of the novel even Stevens himself seems to have recognized that in switching off his moral conscience and handing over his capacities for ethical judgment to another, he abandoned his integrity and lost, to use a word he deploys frequently and makes much of, his dignity. ("'At least [Lord Darlington] had the privilege of being able to say at the end of his life that he made his own mistakes,'" he acknowledges bitterly in the book's closing pages. "'As for myself, I cannot even clam that. You see, I trusted . . . I can't even say I made my own mistakes. Really—one has to ask oneself—what dignity is there in that?'"[16])

The commitment to accept and enthusiastically endorse the decisions of one's superiors, though, is expected as a matter of course in many contexts, including some that might not strike us as being as antiquated as the country house setting in which Ishiguro's novel takes place. Four-star general and former Secretary of State Colin Powell has expressed the following view of what loyalty demands in a military context:

When we are debating an issue, loyalty means giving me your honest opinion, whether you think I'll like it or not. Disagreement, at this stage, stimulates me. But once a decision has been made, the debate ends. From that point on, loyalty means executing the decision as if it were your own.[17]

Defenders of Powell's view might point out that it does allow for debate—at least up to a point. They might observe, too, that while Powell requires that once that debate has been concluded his subordinates ought to execute a decision as if it were their own, he does not say that they must agree with the decision *internally*. But this flexibility may not be as valuable as it might at first appear, for what it seems to do is to place the virtue of loyalty at odds with other virtues, such as honesty and integrity. To demand that a person believe something she knows to be false is to demand something very difficult, if not psychologically impossible. To require that a person acts in a way that she believes to be wrong, or with which she deeply disagrees, is to demand something that might be psychologically possible; but the question of whether it is reasonable is a different matter altogether.

Powell's own conduct with respect to the My Lai massacre is worth mentioning here. As an assistant chief of staff of operations for the Americal Division in Vietnam, Powell was given the task of investigating allegations about My Lai. Powell's findings largely exonerated the American military of wrongdoing or responsibility for the massacre. Powell fulfilled his charge by presenting a nearly unremittingly benign picture of the American military, writing, for example, that "In direct refutation to [Tom Glen's] portrayal is the fact that relations between American soldiers and the Vietnamese people are excellent." In light of the known facts at the time, this assessment can only be regarded as deeply unrealistic, a kind of whitewashing of history—the kind of whitewashing that is no more tolerable for being, as it likely was (and as such acts frequently are), motivated not only by a desire to please his superiors but by genuine and deeply felt patriotic sentiments.

There is a general tension between wholeheartedly loving one's country and acknowledging the truth about it, for the whole truth about any country always contains elements that are difficult for moral persons to accept. As Harry Brighouse writes:

> A good deal of what actually happened makes any country distinctly unlovable to someone possessed of an effective sense of justice. I suspect the conservative patriots in the US are right to want anti-communism, Hiroshima, Watergate, the secret war on Cambodia, and slavery to be glossed over rather quickly . . . The truth is frequently inconvenient and may suffer in pursuit of patriotic sentiment.[18]

This may remind us of Simon Keller's claim that part of being a good friend is "not aiming at the truth" when forming beliefs about that friend. Indeed, Keller has argued that patriotic sentiments involve a similar sort of bias and amount to, in his view, a kind of bad faith.[19]

To what extent are truth and loyalty compatible? There is a range of positions one might take on this issue; but at the very least the tension must be acknowledged. People sometimes use phrases such as "unquestioning loyalty" and "unswerving dedication," but these are two very different ways of praising loyal behavior. If unswerving dedication is simply dedication that does not, in fact, swerve, then someone who showed unswerving dedication might still have been willing to modify her behavior had there been reason to do so—had she discovered, for instance, that the object of her loyalty was not worthy of it. The very idea of unquestioning loyalty, on the other hand, seems to be that one is not open to having one's mind changed or one's loyalty challenged: virtue is shown by one's persistence in a given allegiance, even in the face of contrary evidence, or by one's willingness to perform "difficult" actions, even in the face of one's own moral reservations and hesitations.

Such devotion is often praised; witness the veneration directed toward Hachiko. (We sometimes praise ourselves for it, too, and use such praise to motivate ourselves to overcome our own moral reservations. As Mr. Stevens says of his carrying out Lord Darlington's order to dismiss the Jewish maids: "my duty in this instance was quite clear, and as I saw it, there was nothing to be gained at all in irresponsibly displaying such personal doubts. It was a difficult task, but as such, one that demanded to be carried out with dignity."[20]) But it should never be forgotten how many atrocities have been committed by the unquestioningly loyal, who all too often congratulated themselves afterward for having been, in their own eyes, virtuous enough to perform the hard but necessary acts that their allegiances called on them to perform.

Two

LOYALTY'S UNAVOIDABLE DILEMMAS

Although we sometimes think of this as an age of skepticism, the truth is that almost all of us believe in at least some sorts of moral obligations. There are, of course, quite a few who *claim* to believe that morality is all illusion, and nothing but a sham. But nearly all of these people, in fact, recognize some moral limit or other, both in terms of the actions they could and could not bring themselves to do, and in terms of the types of treatment they would be prepared to tolerate or object to. Moral skepticism is like virtue: it's easy to call yourself a skeptic or a saint—the more difficult task is actually behaving like one.

One type of obligation that most of us believe in is *contractual* obligations: we think we are obligated to keep the promises we have made and abide by the contracts we have voluntarily entered into. And most of us also believe in what I will call obligations of *respect*: we believe, that is, that we, and all people, are bound by negative requirements not to interfere with the lives of others, or to treat them in various other harmful and disrespectful ways.

Skepticism is substantially more common, though, with respect to loyalty obligations. Indeed, loyalty itself strikes many people today as an anachronistic and even somewhat embarrassing notion, a naïve and perhaps childlike "virtue" that we ought, by this point, to have grown beyond and discarded. Part of the reason for this may be that loyalty obligations occupy a territory between contractual obligations and obligations of respect. Like contractual obligations, loyalty obligations are owed to particular persons, and most of them are positive rather than negative: they are obligations *to do* something, and not just to refrain from doing something. But like obligations of respect, many loyalty obligations are not duties we have voluntarily taken upon ourselves; and, indeed, many of them arise from relationships—family relations, citizenship, and so forth—that we did not voluntarily choose.

Of course, this intermediate status does not itself explain why loyalty obligations would be a common object of skepticism: it is not immediately obvious that there is anything dubious about occupying this in-between space. I want to suggest, though, that there is a connection, albeit one that might not be immediately apparent. Much of the resistance to loyalty obligations, I will argue, is rooted in a fear that obligations of this sort threaten moral agency in a way that other obligations do not. The key point has to do with moral dilemmas, and in particular with *unavoidable* moral dilemmas.

Just what is a moral dilemma? In the broadest sense, people sometimes use the word "dilemma" to refer to any difficult decision. In this sense, having to choose between two fulfilling jobs, two pleasant cities of residence, or two desirable romantic partners would count as dilemmas. A more restrictive use applies "dilemma" only to decisions in which there are only *bad* options, so that whatever option you choose, you will to some extent regret it. Choosing between two *good* jobs would not count as a dilemma by this conception, but having to take one of an array of very unpleasant jobs would. Note that both of these types of dilemma may involve regret, as one is forced either to give up a desirable option or to accept an undesirable one.

The second conception takes us much of the way to the idea of particularly *moral* dilemmas, which we will understand as situations in which no matter what one does, one will have done something morally wrong, or at the very least seriously morally questionable—something one should feel uneasy if not downright bad about having done. It is the possibility of a certain sort of moral dilemma—one that is very threatening, in a distinctive way, to the autonomy of moral agents—that seems to be raised by loyalty obligations.

My claim is not that the existence of moral dilemmas depends on the existence of loyalty obligations.[1] They can arise, for instance, out of purely contractual obligations. Suppose that I promise A that I will tend to her invalid mother this weekend, and then without giving it any thought promise B that this weekend I will tend to B's invalid father. And let's suppose, for reasons that I won't bother to spell out, that it is not possible for me to keep both promises. (A's mother and B's father live in separate cities and cannot be moved, etc.) Nor can I afford to simply pay someone to step in and take over for me in one of the cases. (Or perhaps each needs a special form of care that only I can provide.) I cannot keep both promises and so must choose to break at least one, so that the inevitable result is that I wrong someone.

I do not see any good reason for denying that such cases are possible, or for insisting that if I were to break my promise to A, I would not wrong A. (Wishing that the world were not so does not count as a good reason.) The best attempt to deny this might appeal to the popular principle that "ought implies can": since I cannot keep both of these promises—it is simply impossible—it cannot be the case that I ought to, and therefore it cannot be wrong of me to fail to do so. But this misses the mark. Suppose, again, that I keep my promise to B, and so break my promise to A. What I have done wrong is not "to fail to keep both my promises," for this does run afoul of the "ought implies can" requirement. What I have done, rather, is that I have failed to keep my promise to A, and since keeping my promise to A is something I could have done, the requirement to keep that promise does not violate "ought implies can." Of course, doing so would have meant breaking my promise to B, but that does not change the matter. After all, if we imagine that it really *was* impossible for me to keep my promise to A—suppose that I fell into a coma on Friday and did not recover until Tuesday—we can see that the situation would be very different. In this situation A would surely understand my having failed to keep the promise; moreover, it would not count as a *broken* promise. But in the situation in which I *could have* kept the promise but did not (because doing so would have meant breaking a promise to somebody else) A might well react quite differently. "Yes, you would have had to break your promise to someone else to keep your promise to me," she might say, "but my point is simply this: for whatever reason, you chose not to keep a promise that you made to me and could have kept."

We should accept, then, that there can be moral dilemmas. Notice, though, that a feature of this case, as I have described it, is that this was in no way an *unavoidable* dilemma. It is quite clear that I could have avoided it, simply by refraining from making two mutually incompatible promises. While dilemmas tend to strike us as unpleasant and disturbing, we should nonetheless admit their possibility; but this is not *deeply* disturbing, so long as the dilemmas are avoidable. It is significant, then, that the example above concerned *voluntarily assumed* moral obligations. Because such obligations are voluntarily assumed, these obligations, and the dilemmas that they can create, are avoidable: we can avoid being placed in a dilemma situation by being careful about what we promise. I want to suggest that what really makes us uncomfortable is not the possibility of dilemmas, but the possibility of *unavoidable* dilemmas: dilemmas, that is, that are created by a conflict of obligations that are placed on us without, so to speak, our permission.

It is precisely this possibility—the possibility of un-avoidable dilemmas—that is opened up by loyalty. For loyalty, as ordinarily understood, at least sometimes generates obligations that are non-voluntary, and so in a deep sense unavoidable. The standard account seems to have it that I have obligations to my country, and also to my parents, siblings, and other relatives; and none of these were communities or persons whom I chose to be obligated toward. But it is also clear that loyalty can generate obligations that conflict. If loyalty works the way it is commonly thought to, then it is clear that it at least has the potential to generate unavoidable dilemmas. If my relationship to my country requires me to do x, my relationship with my brother requires me to do y, and I cannot do both x and y, then I am in a genuine and deep moral dilemma. (We might imagine, for instance, that my brother has committed some crime, for which the law demands I turn him in.) But since I did not choose these relationships, or voluntarily assume these obligations, the dilemma is not at all avoidable in the sense that the dilemma above, which resulted from my having made incompatible voluntary promises, was avoidable. No amount of being careful and attentive with regard to the promises I make and the obligations I assume will keep me clear of dilemmas of this sort. All I can do, it seems, is hope that I am lucky enough never to find myself in one.

I suspect it is the fact that loyalty, at least as commonly understood, tends to generate unavoidable dilemmas that lies at the root of much of the suspicion that some people feel toward its alleged obligations. As I said above, it is not merely that loyalty obligations are non-voluntary; most people are willing to accept the existence of many non-voluntary moral obligations—obligations of respect, for instance. Nor is it merely the fact that it sometimes generates dilemmas; again, moral dilemmas can arise out of contractual obligations alone. But the idea of non-voluntary and, hence, unavoidable dilemmas—dilemmas that one did not place oneself in through one's voluntary actions—seems deeply problematic in a more serious and more disturbing way.

Socrates was fond of claiming that the only truly bad thing that could befall a person was that he might lose his good character. Any other loss, he sometimes suggested, could be tolerated; but the loss of one's good character would be the loss of the most valuable thing one could possibly possess. And in Socrates's view, it was up to us whether we lived well or not, which meant that it was up to us whether we kept our good characters or not. In his view, then, the only thing that truly harms us is something that we can always choose, by conscientious living, to avoid. But the idea of unavoidable moral dilemmas casts doubt on this optimistic view. If it is possible, no matter what you do or how you live, to find yourself in such a dilemma, then it seems that it is possible that the world might place you, through no fault of your own, in a situation in which no matter what you do you will end up suffering the greatest harm a human being can suffer—a harm inflicted on your moral character itself. No wonder some people feel such a strong resistance to the idea that our loyalties can obligate us in way that we do not control, and in ways which, at the end of the day, might require incompatible and, hence, impossible things of us.

IMPARTIALITY AND COMPLICITY: "DON'T ASK ME TO TIE THE ROPE"

Not every apparent conflict of loyalties represents an actual conflict: some apparent cases of deep conflict can be explained away. Consider the conscientious objector who refuses to take part in a war he regards as unjustified and immoral. Such a person is *disobedient*, but not *disloyal*; what he does is not a betrayal of his country. Nor is he a bad citizen. Indeed, the very ideas of civil disobedience and conscientious objection seem to contain the thought that such forms of disobedience are at times justified, not only by abstract moral considerations but, one hopes, by the ideals that have guided one's country at its best moments and ought to do so here. (It is important that such opposition be open and principled: the attempt is not to evade justice, but to force a change. As Martin Luther King formulated the requirement: "One who breaks an unjust law must do so openly, lovingly, and with a willingness to accept the penalty.") The conscientious objector might be seen as part of the "loyal opposition," one of the citizens who is willing to oppose his country's current projects and pursuits, which he regards as misguided, in the attempt to return it to a more admirable course.

It is surely too optimistic, though, to hope that every apparent loyalty dilemma can be explained away with no tragic residue. In short story writer André Dubus's "A Father's Story," Luke Ripley chooses to protect his daughter by concealing the fact that, while driving, she has struck and killed a pedestrian.[2] There are multiple ambiguities in the story, some of which Ripley cannot himself resolve. Did the fact that his daughter had had a few drinks contribute to the accident, or was it the victim's fault for being on the wrong side of the road? Might the victim, who lived long enough to drag himself out of the road, have survived if Ripley's daughter, or Ripley himself, had reported the accident immediately? What Ripley does know is that what he has done cannot be morally justified, and that in hiding his daughter's accident from the authorities he has severed himself from his community. ("I stood and turned into the wind," he tells us, "slid down the ditch and crawled out of it, and went up the hill and down it, across the road to the street of houses whose people I had left behind forever, so that I moved with stealth in the shadows to my truck."[3]) In choosing to shield his daughter he is distancing himself from his identity as a member of that community—along with his religious commitments, which would have had him behave quite differently, according to the precepts of impartial justice—in favor of something more fundamental, his identity as a father:

> Now in the mornings while I watch purple finches driving larger titmice from the feeder, I say to [God]: I would do it again. For when she knocked on my door, then called me, she woke what had flowed dormant in my blood since her birth, so that what rose from the bed was not a stable owner or a Catholic or any other Luke Ripley I had lived with for a long time, but the father of a girl.[4]

We sometimes speak of having to decide "where one's loyalty lies." But this phrase simplifies the situation in a way by making loyalty singular rather than plural. It is more accurate to say, of a person like Luke Ripley, that he had to decide which of his loyalties to act on, and which of his loyalties he would betray. To decide this is to decide to attach oneself to one among the many roles that one plays in life, and thus to decide, in a deep sense, who one really is.

Such decisions are morally profound. It would be a deep mistake to think that since anything one does in a dilemma is to some extent wrong, it therefore does not matter how one chooses, or that one can proceed after having chosen with a clear and comfortable conscience, as if nothing morally serious has happened. One ought to feel regret for what one has done; one should suffer the pangs of conscience. To do otherwise—to let oneself off the hook by focusing on the fact that *some* sort of wrongdoing was, in the circumstances, unavoidable—would be a shallow type of response. Perhaps, then, what matters most in such cases is the way in which we conduct ourselves afterward, how we respond to the tragic residue, and whether we are adult enough to let ourselves admit that the residue is tragic and that we can never be fully reconciled to it. We did have a choice: avoiding wrong was not an option, but avoiding the particular wrong that was committed was. Luke Ripley, for his part, knows that he has done wrong, and he does not hide from this fact, nor does he seek the solace of an easy expiation:

> That was the time to say I want to confess, but I have not and will not. Though I could now, for Jennifer is in Florida, and weeks have passed, and perhaps now Father Paul would not feel that he must tell me to go to the police. And, for that very reason, to confess now would be unfair. It is a world of secrets, and now I have one from my best, in truth my only, friend. I have one from Jennifer, too, but that is the nature of fatherhood.[5]

What Luke Ripley faces in "A Father's Story" is an existential choice, a choice of what kind of person one will be, of what role one will choose to identify with. By choosing to protect his daughter, he chooses to stand with a particular individual as opposed to the larger, and somewhat abstract, community. This description in itself risks making the choice seem too abstract: it is important both that he chooses to protect a *particular* individual, and that the primary victim may be another particular individual, the accident victim who, for all we know, might have lived had Ripley contacted the authorities immediately.

Such choices, according to Jean-Paul Sartre, cannot be settled by appeal to some universal theory of ethics. Sartre offers an example that has become famous, that of a young student who had to choose between taking care of his mother (who had been abandoned by her husband and whose other son had perished in the war) or abandoning her to join the Free French Forces. About this case Sartre writes the following:

> What could help him make that choice? The Christian doctrine? No. The Christian doctrine tells us we must be charitable, love our neighbor, sacrifice ourselves for others, choose the "narrow way," et cetera. But what is the narrow way? Whom should we love like a brother—the soldier or the mother? Which is the more useful aim—the vague one of fighting as part of a group, or the more concrete one of helping one particular person keep on living? Who can decide that *a priori*? No one. No code of ethics on record answers that question. Kantian morality instructs us to never treat another as a means, but always as an end. Very well; therefore, if I stay with my mother, I will treat her as an end, not as a means. But by the same token,

I will be treating those who are fighting on my behalf as a means. Conversely, if I join those who are fighting, I will treat them as an end, and, in so doing, risk treating my mother as a means.[6]

Sartre suggests that in making a choice of this sort, we are choosing for all of humanity: "in confronting any real situation ... I bear the responsibility of a choice that, in committing myself, also commits humanity as a whole."[7] But this seems mistaken: I see no indication that Ripley thinks of himself, or needs to think of himself, as making a decision that would somehow be mandatory for any human being in that situation. (Indeed, Ripley suggests that he himself would probably have chosen differently if his child had been a son rather than a daughter.) His choice is, rather, a personal decision: it is not clear that he would pass judgment on a person in a similar situation who made the opposite choice— who chose, that is, to prioritize his role as a citizen over his role as a father.

The newspaper columnist Anna Quindlen recently wrote: "I would be fully prepared to lie under oath if I considered it to be the best thing for my kid. I would consider that a more moral position than telling the truth. And I am certain I am in the majority."[8] Quindlen's justification appeals to the value of trust that ought to obtain between family members: the legal requirement to testify against one's children, she writes, would undermine that trust, and so represent an unfortunate intrusion of the public interest into the private sphere. "A Father's Story" might help make such considerations vivid. Suppose that Jennifer had been certain that her father would report her when she approached him after the accident— would she not, then, have felt compelled to hide it from him as well as from everyone else? And what does family life become—what would it have been for Jennifer and her father, even before the accident, even if the accident had never happened—when children do not feel that they can trust their parents to put their own needs and interests over more abstract considerations?

It is also important to keep in mind that in "A Father's Story" it is not clear that Jennifer has done anything wrong. It seems at least likely that the accident in question really was a genuine *accident*, in the deepest sense—a random, uncontrollable occurrence of which Jennifer, as much as the man she hit, is an innocent victim. On the other hand, she did drink a number of beers before attempting to drive home. The reader cannot know, any more than Luke Ripley can, whether this contributed to the accident. Nor is it made clear whether the man she hit would have survived if Luke Ripley had contacted the authorities immediately. But we should keep in mind, of course, that even if her drinking *did* contribute to the accident, the accident would still be, in an important way, a result of bad luck. It was her bad luck that on that particular night there happened to be a person in that particular spot on the road at precisely the wrong moment. Another person, or Jennifer herself on another night, might have had as many or more drinks and driven with just the same degree of care, and made it home entirely safely.

This contribution of luck to the situation is surely one of the considerations lying behind Luke Ripley's decision to protect his daughter. Had she plotted and carried out the murder of an innocent man, the temptation to protect his daughter from justice would not have struck him with the same overriding force, and might not have been felt at all. The fact that she did not intend to harm anyone, and that she not only regrets but will likely be shattered by the fact that she did, and that it is in large part bad luck that brought about this outcome, all lead Ripley to view Jennifer as, in an important sense, morally innocent. In the abstract, many of us are content to support laws and policies that would punish individuals who are just as innocent. (Otherwise our laws regarding drunk driving, negligent manslaughter, etc. would have a very different shape.) But when it is one's own child who stands to be punished, things may suddenly seem very different indeed.

What I am suggesting is that the reasoning that lies behind Luke Ripley's decision, and behind whatever inclination the reader may feel to find that decision intelligible, consists in part in a skepticism not just about our criminal justice system as it currently exists, but about the very idea of impartial justice, the idea that *any* impartial and impersonal system that society might devise could dispense justice in a manner that recognizes and is consistent with the needs of human individuals. The justice system we have, and perhaps any that we could imagine implementing, is, of necessity, a compromise, motivated as much by the need to discourage social misbehavior and to maintain security as by the desire to treat individual people as they actually deserve to be treated. And what loving father would want to place his daughter in the hands of such a system? "Then I threw the cigarette and hope both out the window," Ripley tells us, "and prayed that he was alive, while beneath the prayer, a reserve deeper in my heart, another one stirred: that if he were dead, they would not get Jennifer."[9]

What Ripley's loyalty to his daughter does is to make the situation personal. His attachment to his daughter deeply affects the way in which Ripley conceives of the situation: the demands of impartial justice, not to mention the needs of vulnerable strangers (here, the accident victim), still register in Ripley's mind, but with considerably less motivational force than they normally would. On the other hand, because it is his daughter in danger and not some stranger, he has a much more vivid apprehension of her vulnerability and of what she might suffer at the hands of the justice system.

There is another way, too, in which Ripley's loyalty makes the situation personal. Let us suppose that despite what I said above, Ripley nonetheless judged that the best possible outcome was that the authorities were contacted about the accident—an outcome that would inevitably include Jennifer being brought to face some sort of justice. A father in his position might acknowledge this to be so, and yet still resist acting so as to bring this best outcome about, precisely because, in light of his relationship with his daughter, he does not want to be the one who brings it about. Such a father would recognize that, in some larger sense, justice ought to be served. Perhaps he would not stand in the way of someone else who was determined to bring about this outcome. But because bringing it about that justice be done would involve the suffering of his daughter, he himself would want no part of it; he would strongly desire not to be the instrument of the harm that is to be visited upon her.

We see an example of this in the film The Third Man (Carol Reed, 1949), in the relationship between Holly Martins (Joseph Cotton) and Harry Lime (Orson Welles). Martins and Lime were friends years ago, and Martins feels a loyalty to Lime that persists throughout much of the film. Eventually, though, his associate, Major Calloway (Trevor Howard), manages to convince Martins that Lime is guilty of selling defective penicillin on the black market, resulting in the death of many meningitis-afflicted children. Martins now realizes that he can no longer be Lime's friend, or defend his innocence. Yet he still feels a certain loyalty, for when Calloway suggests a scheme by which Lime might be apprehended, Martins replies: "Calloway, you expect too much. I know he deserves to hang, you proved your stuff. But twenty years is a long time—don't ask me to tie the rope."

Some would claim, perhaps, not to understand such an attitude, or would insist that it could not be rational. Given that the harm is going to be inflicted on your friend one way or the other—and that it *should* be inflicted, that he *deserves* to suffer—what difference does it make that you rather than someone else are the instrument of its happening? Doesn't your desire not to be the instrument reduce to nothing more than a concern for the cleanness of one's own hands and the purity of one's own conscience, one's ability to sleep at night untroubled (or not as troubled) by regret and remorse? This feeling is compounded in the case of The Third Man by the fact that Lime's actions are morally egregious (Martins is taken to see some of the suffering children, and while the audience does not see them, we see his reactions, which is enough), and also by the fact that Lime's own conscience seems to be entirely untroubled by what he has done.

The skeptical doubts that one might feel about this notion of integrity are not, then, unintelligible. Even so, this feeling— the desire not to be an agent of harm to someone whom one loves, even though the harm will happen regardless—is such a deep and robust element of our moral psychology that it seems unlikely we could overcome it even if we were to decide that it is thoroughly irrational. And if it is somewhat unclear in The Third Man that Martins's qualms can be justified, the same cannot, perhaps, be said about "A Father's Story." To ask that a father deliver his own daughter into the hands of a flawed and frequently brutal justice system to be punished for a crime of carelessness—a "crime" that resulted from behavior no worse than that which thousands of people engage in every day—is to ask too much, or rather, to ask the wrong sort of thing, from a person who feels the sort of loyalty toward his family that a father ought to feel.

THE PLURALITY OF LOYALTIES AND
THE DISUNITY OF THE VIRTUES

Precisely what sorts of dilemmas loyalty can lead to is a matter of some disagreement: different theories of moral obligation will give different answers. However, any but the most minimal account will imply that loyalties at least sometimes conflict in a serious way. Loyalty may be a single virtue, but because we have multiple loyalties it tends to attach us to a plurality of values, some of which may conflict with others.

How are such conflicts to be resolved? The simplest view would be one that divided loyalties into different types—perhaps in virtue of their objects—and asserted that some types consistently outranked others. Thus, one might hold that loyalty to one's country always outweighed loyalty to one's family (or vice versa), that loyalty to one's spouse always outweighed loyalty to one's children (or vice versa), and so forth. But there is no obvious or generally agreed-upon hierarchy of loyalties that could systematically settle such matters. Indeed, even putting aside disagreement *between* different people about which loyalties should prevail over which others, what seems clear is that our judgments about these matters are *particular* – that is, case-by-case judgments: it is not generally true that any class of loyalties should always take priority over all or some others.

Some moral theories can happily allow for this. Utilitarianism, for instance, holds that the morally right action is always the one that brings about the best possible consequences in terms of general well-being. So protecting one's daughter would be right where that maximized general well-being, and refusing to protect her would be right where *that* maximized general well-being. But while utilitarianism can allow that conflicts of loyalty need to be decided on a case-by-case basis, which is what reflection on cases of actual conflict seems to suggest, the considerations that it takes to be relevant in making that determination are not at all the same considerations that actual moral agents tend to consider. Luke Ripley's deliberations, for instance, seem to have little if anything to do with the matter of what would be best for people, in general, or for society at large, and the fact that this is so is part of what renders "A Father's Story" such a realistic depiction. Utilitarianism does not allow ties of loyalty to bear any intrinsic moral weight at all; if such ties are ever good, they are only good instrumentally – that is, good in so far as respecting them leads people to do the thing that is morally right (but right for reasons that have nothing to do with loyalty).

The other main objection to utilitarianism in this context emerges from Sartre's point that major moral theories are simply not of much use in resolving dilemmas of this sort. The defining feature of such dilemmas is that there are very compelling reasons for, and very compelling reasons against, each of the available options here, and whichever option the agent chooses will, if he is morally sensitive at all, leave him with a considerable amount of regret and remorse. And this is not a feature that Kantianism (the example Sartre explicitly mentions) or utilitarianism can comfortably accommodate.

Both of these theories imply that there is a right thing to do in such a situation, that doing the best one can do is always, morally speaking, good enough, and that because doing the best one can do is good enough, it should leave no deep regret or moral remainder.

From the fact that there is no overarching objective theory of ethics that can resolve such dilemmas for us, it might be tempting to leap to the conclusion that there are no objectively true ethical claims at all, and perhaps to a kind of nihilism according to which the only values and moral reasons are the ones we ourselves make up or endorse. This seems to be Sartre's view, at least sometimes: he often speaks, for instance, as if it is always true that *every* available option is equal in value, as when he writes that "Everything has the same value, whether it be writing [Dostoevski's] *The Possessed* or drinking a cup of coffee."[10] And sometimes he goes still further, suggesting that, since human life is absurd, no option possesses *any* value: all available options, actions, and outcomes are valueless.

But, in fact, these nihilistic views are not presupposed by, and do not follow from, the picture we have been drawing of loyalty dilemmas, and it is important to see why. For one thing, we might not want to say that the student's problem is that the two options he is trying to choose between (joining the resistance or taking care of his mother) are equal in value. It might be better, for various reasons, to say that they are *incomparable*, and that for this reason one cannot rationally decide between them.[11] Even if we do prefer to say that they are equal in value, we surely do not want to say that *all* options are equal in value. (If the student faced a three-way choice between joining the resistance, taking care of his mother, or having a cup of coffee, it would be clear which would be the first to go.) Finally, the idea that no option has *any* value is very hard to square with the fact that this choice is a *dilemma*: indeed, the idea that a choice represents a dilemma seems to imply that the options do have some sort of value, for otherwise it would not be worth agonizing about. I can hardly place you in a dilemma by offering you the choice between a 1978 penny and a 1979 penny. Indeed, to realize that none of the options from which one must choose bears any significant value at all might well occasion a sigh of relief, for the effect of this realization would be to *release* one from what might previously have appeared to be a dilemma.

In a sense, then, there are limits to how deep dilemmas in a truly nihilistic world can be. For in such a world nothing has any real value, and a choice between various valueless options is hardly a dilemma in the most profound sense: regardless of one's choice one could not rationally regret it (since whatever one gave up would have been worthless in its own right). This, however, does not seem to be the sort of world we live in. Rather, we seem to live in a world in which values are real but plural: they compete and conflict, at least at times, so that we moral agents are sometimes faced with the regrettable necessity of having to decide which to promote or honor, and which to sacrifice. And it may be that, no matter which one we choose, we will have a hard time living with the choice. Moreover, as the case of conflicting loyalties already suggests, this is not simply because choosing the better option— indeed, choosing *either* option—may nonetheless involve an uncompensated loss. It is because we may find ourselves in still more unpleasant cases, cases in which, no matter what one does, one will have done something *wrong*. For it is not only values but the virtues themselves that are pluralistic and thus divided against themselves.

To say that the virtues are "divided against themselves" can signal one of two types of conflict. The first type of conflict involves virtues that conflict with one another. Think of situations, for instance, in which the honest thing to do is not the kind thing to do. Or cases in which justice demands an uncharitable action (like refusing to forgive someone, or delivering a benefit to the person who is entitled to it rather than the person who could make the best use of it). Loyalty frequently enters into such conflicts: it can demand that you lie or conceal a truth, or turn your back on those who fall outside the border that defines your family, your tribe, or your country. The virtues do not always harmonize in their demands: there are cases in which they oppose each other, in which loyalty to family, for instance, is incompatible with honesty, or with the demands of justice.

The other sort of conflict involves a single virtue divided against itself. It is not clear whether this sort of conflict is possible with respect to every sort of virtue. Perhaps it is hard to imagine a situation in which the same action is courageous or wise in one sense, but not in another. But we can probably imagine a situation in which one and the same action is kind to one person but not to another. And there is no difficulty whatsoever with the concept of an action that is loyal to one person (country, etc.) but not another. In an ideal world, perhaps it would be somehow guaranteed that legitimate loyalties could never conflict, so that in cases of conflicting loyalties it would always be possible, at least in principle, to find and act on the loyalty whose demands were endorsed by morality, and whose legitimacy thus dissolved or rendered inert the demands made by the attachments it opposed. Again, though, the world that we live in does not appear to be ideal, or even close to ideal, in this way.

Cases of loyalty provide numerous examples of situations in which a person, to borrow a phrase from Philippa Foot, "can only become good in one way by being bad in another."[12] Suppose one's brother is the Unabomber—what does one do? One must either betray one's brother or be a bad citizen, just as Sartre's student had to choose either to betray his mother or betray the Resistance. Those who find themselves in such situations are not necessarily responsible for being there, and the way they choose to respond will not say *everything* there is to say about their characters: part of the reason that moral dilemmas trouble us the way they do is that the deepest emotion we experience in response to them—a profound regret at being forced to choose between two awful alternatives—is not itself an emotion that can be effectively or usefully expressed by any of the actions we might choose to perform. (That, indeed, is precisely why we feel that regret so keenly). Nonetheless, while the choice you make in a dilemma will not say everything there is to say about you as a moral agent, what it does say will be profound. Even if you were in no way responsible for finding yourself trapped between two unattractive if not intolerable alternatives, it is nonetheless entirely possible that the decision that you make will end up haunting you for the remainder of your life. All that philosophy can do here is to help us admit the reality of such dilemmas; it cannot dissolve them or grant us a magic key that would somehow let us avoid them.

Loyalty, Tribalism, Violence

Three

THE EVOLUTION OF LOYALTY

Like nearly every human phenomenon, loyalty-exhibiting behavior results from a complex interplay of nature and culture. Nature helps to determine our general motivational character and behavioral tendencies, at least at "ground level." But those tendencies can be encouraged or discouraged, and developed or repressed in various complex ways by one's society and upbringing. The question of just how much of a contribution each one makes, and just how much "human nature" is susceptible to being shaped and molded by culture, remains a matter of ongoing debate; but we can say with considerable confidence that to ignore the contribution of either nature or culture would be a grave mistake.

Nature provides the raw human materials that culture gets to work with. The question to ask, then, is why human individuals would have evolved to contain and manifest various tendencies toward forms of loyal behavior—tendencies, for instance, to become attached to other individuals, to small groups of individuals, and to larger communities of whom they are members. The answer is not too mysterious, at least in broad outline. It is that such tendencies would be expected, in at least most environments (including the ones our ancestors evolved in) to provide an evolutionary advantage—to make it more likely, that is, that the genes of the individuals that manifested these traits would be passed on to succeeding generations.

Initially there may seem to be a puzzle here. Many loyalty-related behaviors, as we have seen, involve self-sacrifice: to be loyal is, in part, to be willing to sacrifice one's interests, up to and sometimes including sacrificing one's very life, for the benefit of the loyalty object. But how could the willingness to sacrifice oneself be an evolutionary advantage? Surely, it might be thought, the tendency to self-sacrifice is a huge disadvantage in the evolutionary lottery: those creatures that are programmed to neglect their own interests for the sake of others will be far less likely to pass on their genes than those creatures that are programmed to look out for number one at all times. We all know that self-promoting individualism tends to pay off in the economic free market; should we not expect it to pay off in the market of natural selection as well?

But this line of thought is not as convincing as it may at first appear. First, while loyalty does involve a certain willingness to sacrifice oneself, it is at least possible that the evolutionary costs of that tendency will be more than compensated, even at the level of the individual. It might be, first, that in many environments the individual, though psychologically willing to sacrifice herself for the sake of the community, will not actually be called upon to do so. If so, then the costs of having this tendency might be fairly minimal. At the same time, this tendency might have various salutary effects. Suppose, for instance, that individuals who are inclined to loyalty therefore find it easier to form emotional attachments with others of their species: they are more open, more trusting, more generous, and so forth. If so, then these individuals might be more attractive than their more selfish counterparts, and so have an easier time finding mates. And in the evolutionary lottery, for sexual beings like ourselves, being able to find a mate is the biggest advantage there is: indeed, a creature that does not manage to mate will not reproduce, and so is automatically a loser—a Darwinian dead-end—in evolutionary terms.

This is an important lesson to keep in mind when thinking about evolution: what matters from this perspective is not how long you live or how much success or pleasure you enjoy in your individual existence, but whether your genes get passed on—and, moreover, passed on to creatures who will be able to pass them on in turn. This has huge implications for creatures like us, for the crucial reason that human beings go through an extended period of infancy during which we need to be taken care of by others—typically, by our parents. A newborn human will not survive on its own, which means that those humans who do survive will need someone who is motivated enough—that is, altruistic enough—to provide a certain level of childcare. From the perspective of the genes, then—and again, this is the perspective that matters when we are considering which traits get replicated and distributed, and which others tend to decrease with time, if not vanish altogether—a tendency to a certain level of altruism is clearly, in many contexts, an advantage.

Of course, it is not clear that the tendency to sacrifice oneself for the benefit of any other creature, or even any other human, would be an advantage, any more than the tendency to sacrifice oneself for no reason at all would be. From the gene's point of view, the optimal strategy would be for individuals to be willing to undergo a certain level of sacrifice for the individuals who carry their genes—their children, most obviously, but also their siblings (since they carry "their" genes in the relevant sense) and, to a lesser degree, other relatives as well. As R. Paul Shaw and Yuwa Wong write:

> . . . genetic fitness has not one but two basic components to be maximized. The first is increased personal survival and increased personal reproduction (classical Darwinian fitness). The second is the enhanced reproduction and survival of close relatives who share the same genes by common descent (a kinship component) . . . Kin selection implies that sexual organisms, such as humans, have evolved not only to be egoistic but to be fundamentally nepotistically altruistic.[1]

What we should expect, then, is that over time evolution will encourage the tendency, among creatures like ourselves, to be biased in favor of people who we are (or take ourselves to be) related to—which is precisely what the empirical evidence tends to suggest. Thus, evolutionary psychology helps to explain why we are creatures with proclivities toward forming certain sorts of attachments. At the same time, basic biological facts about human beings help to explain why we *need* such attachments. Human beings, again, are extraordinarily vulnerable in the early stages of life, and hence extremely dependent on others. Without the devoted care and attention of our parents, we simply would not survive. And even in later stages of life we frequently find ourselves dependent to some considerable degree on various forms of support from the individuals who surround us.

A lengthy stage of dependence and vulnerability is bound to leave its psychological mark on adult human beings. Adult humans typically manifest a deep-seated need for relationships of trust, and tend to feel radically insecure in the absence of such relationships, or when what appeared to be a relationship of this sort reveals itself as something else. As Gregory Bateson writes, human beings, like mammals in general:

> . . . are concerned with patterns of relationship, with where they stand in love, hate, respect, dependency, trust and similar abstractions vis-à-vis somebody else. This is where it hurts us to be put in the wrong. If we trust and find that that which we have trusted was untrustworthy . . . we feel *bad*. The pain that human beings and all other mammals can suffer from this type of error is extreme.[2]

Trust and sensitivity to betrayal thus become fairly basic components in the emotional structure of the human individual. We rely on the people around us in a great many ways for a great many things, and in order to flourish, a human being needs the people around her to be people she can trust—to be, that is, people who will not be disloyal to her. That we rely on people in this way, that we need not to be betrayed, is a deep fact about our social nature, and it is reflected in our psychology, in the anxiety we feel at the thought of being abandoned, shunned, or betrayed. Understanding how much this matters in our own case, we find it easy to extend this understanding to others, and are naturally inclined to protect them, much as we desire to protect ourselves, from betrayal and abandonment.

THE LIFE OF THE COMMUNITY

The empirical facts about how human beings have developed, then, are entirely pertinent to the issue of what normative reasons there are to treat them in certain ways and, thus, what normative reasons there are to be loyal to persons. For if human beings were not vulnerable to betrayal in the way that they are—if they did not tend to rely on each other's trustworthiness in quite fundamental ways and to suffer significantly when that trust turned out to be misplaced—trustworthiness and loyalty would not be valued and coveted, nor praised and admired, as they are in the world in which we live.

It will be noted that there are contexts to which this account, as a partial justification for loyalty and a partial explanation of loyalty's importance and value, does not apply. If we have reason to be loyal to entities larger than individual human beings—cities, countries, nations, corporations, clubs, and so forth—it cannot be for this sort of reason, for these entities do not, after all, experience the pain of betrayal in the way that individual human beings do.

What types of normative justification might be available in these contexts, then? One type is simply pragmatic. Institutions cannot prosper if the individuals who compose them are not prepared to engage in certain forms of loyalty-displaying behavior—carrying out "its" decisions even when one disagrees with them, refusing to abandon it when it enters a period of decline, and so forth. After all, as Albert Hirschman points out in Exit, Voice, and Loyalty, nearly every institution will make some decisions that some individual members will disagree with, and nearly every institution will, at some point, go through a period of decline which, with luck, will turn out to be temporary.[3] Since at least many of our institutions make considerable contributions to our well-being, it follows that the health of our social life is to a considerable extent dependent on such behaviors.

But if such commitments of loyalty are necessary to the flourishing of our social life, it should by now be obvious that they also raise grave dangers. Suppose that the company one works for begins issuing directives that one disagrees with, not just because one thinks they are bad for business or otherwise imprudent, but because they are morally objectionable. Should one show one's loyalty by carrying out those directives, hoping that the decision-makers eventually come to their senses? What if the institution one works for is the U.S. military, where one is expected, in the words of Colin Powell, to execute every decision, once it has been made, "as if it were your own"? What if the order is to kill unarmed Vietnamese civilians, to participate in the fire-bombing of a German city, or to torture a prisoner whom one's commanding officers suspect has terrorist ties?

Particularly, perhaps, where the object of loyalty is one's country, the temptation to ignore the ordinary rules of morality and even simple decency can be hard to resist. Moreover, like other forms of loyalty, patriotic attachments can alter one's very perception of the situation one faces, causing one to fail to realize that one *is* ignoring or contravening ordinary rules of morality. (Many Americans who are horrified by torture when other countries practice it seem to regard it as reasonable and acceptable when it is carried out by their own government.) From the perspective of societies that issue demands in the name of loyalty, the ability to do so is often more than a matter of mere convenience. Sometimes, as when a country is under attack and must appeal to the loyalty of its citizens to rise to its defense, the ability to issue such demands and have them met can be literally a matter of survival. Countries that are unable convincingly to make such demands will be unlikely, in the long run, to prosper or even to endure. Thus, nearly all societies actively encourage and strengthen their members' biologically instilled tendencies to form loyalty attachments—sometimes at the level of the family, sometimes at the level of the state. Indeed, many philosophers, beginning with Plato, have argued that getting citizens to develop attachments to their state was one of the primary functions of society.

Thus, the existence of loyalty, and in particular the sort of loyalty that drives people to take up arms, put on uniforms, and try to kill the people on "the other side," needs to be explained on a couple of different levels. On the one hand, the inherent proclivity of individual human beings to engage in loyalty-displaying behaviors is largely to be explained by the fact that possessing tendencies to exhibit such behavior is genetically advantageous (that is, advantageous to the gene, if not to the individual organism that carries the gene). On the other hand, since it is advantageous to societies to have loyal citizens—citizens who will defend their society against threats and do the often difficult and sometimes dangerous work that is necessary to defend it—successful societies will tend to be those that have developed means of encouraging these tendencies in their citizens. Societies that learn to instill patriotic sentiments and attachments of loyalty in their constituent members will tend to survive and flourish, while those unable to do so may, at least under certain conditions, tend toward dissolution and disintegration.

Societies promote such sentiments through diverse means: the media, the educational system, religious institutions, ceremonies, and holidays. The psychological mechanisms being appealed to, meanwhile, include and are centered on the needs and vulnerabilities discussed in the previous section. If the sensitivity to being betrayed is a fundamental element of our emotional constitution, so too is the need to belong, to be part of a community in whom one has a place that renders one's life both intelligible and secure. We remain deeply shaped by the fact that our ancestors were tribal creatures, and one element of this is that we generally need communities in order to prosper; we need to know where we belong, who our relatives are, and who is likely to be there for us when the chips are down.

This is a question not just of security, but of meaning, for one's community memberships almost inevitably form a crucial element of the narratives one tells oneself in constructing one's identity and in trying to achieve self-understanding.[4] Moreover it allows one to tell a different kind of narrative about oneself—a narrative that is larger and broader, and not as contingent on one's individual fortunes; a kind of narrative that helps us to meet the need for "self transcendence" identified by Ernest Partridge. We have already noted that there is a sense in which being a member of a community to which one is loyal enlarges one's life and expands one's horizons, allowing one to share and participate in achievements and triumphs that are entirely beyond one as an individual. Human beings are social by nature, and one of the great goods of sociality is that it lets one fully occupy a much larger world than one could as an isolated individual. But in order to fully enjoy the benefits of community membership, one's attachment to that community must be deep: it must constitute, in a very real way, part of one's identity, thus opening the door to the sentiments and perceived obligations of loyalty.

The community in question, which is often one's society, nation, or culture, is often perceived as an entity whose existence precedes one's existence as an individual and will, barring cataclysm, continue to exist after the individual has died. The result of this is that what societies frequently offer their faithful citizens, implicitly and sometimes explicitly, is not just a further enlargement of their existence, but a kind of immortality. "Consider, for example," writes Avner de-Shalit, "how many diaries, books of poems, collections of letters, etc. have been published posthumously, 'in memory of . . . .' This is our attempt to leave future generations the achievements of our creative self, thereby ensuring that a part of this self will still exist in the future . . . one's thoughts and ideas can still exist beyond physical annihilation, and in this way some part of the fear of death is overcome."[5] For her part, Yael Tamir is explicit in linking the promise of immortality with the demand that citizens sometimes risk death: "The importance of endowing the state with a national task that creates a link between the present generation, its ancestors, and future generations cannot be overstated; it helps individuals conquer the fear of death by promising them an opportunity to enter the sphere of the eternal."[6]

The point of helping citizens to "conquer the fear of death," on Tamir's account, is precisely to encourage them to be willing to risk death, in defense of their country, and to inflict death on those identified as enemies or threats to it. We might wonder whether a rational individual will not see through this attempt to replace one's own good with the good of one's country—many of us, indeed, will hope that they do—but this is precisely where social pressure and appeals to belonging, and the fear of not belonging, are supposed to do their work:

> Yet individuals who adopt a national project may still prefer that others defend the nation-state for them. Freeriding is especially tempting as the existence of a state is a collective good whose benefits individuals would enjoy even if they did not personally contribute to its defense. Commemoration rites and national ceremonies are meant to solve this

collective action problem—namely, to convince individuals that they ought to *commit themselves* to protecting their state with their lives. In venerating and remembering the fallen, the state conveys to its citizens the following message: in committing yourself to the welfare, endurance, security, and prosperity of your state, a commitment that may force you to face danger and risk death, you will secure substantial gains; refraining from such a commitment will, on the other hand, entail social costs.[7]

Those least likely to "free-ride"—those, that is, who are most willing to kill and die for their country (or nation, religion, or cause)—will be those who believe either that dying gloriously as part of an armed struggle against evil is *literally* a guarantee of immortality, as some religions teach, or who accept a variant of the civic religion which claims that the country, or the nation, has a life of its own—a life which, in the long run, matters more than that of any individual member. Pope Pius II held that it was sometimes the case that "for the benefit of the whole body a foot or a hand, which in the state are the citizens, must be amputated."[8] A similar view was expressed by "Sandie" Pendleton, Stonewall Jackson's right-hand staff officer, in a letter to his father from 1862. "Our men are thinking too much of a whole skin, and too little of their country and the future. What difference does a few hours more or less here of life make in comparison with the future destiny of the people?"[9]

This idea, that individuals matter less than the nations or countries of which they are members or citizens, has been massively influential. Perhaps it is important at this juncture, then, to remind ourselves that countries and nations are nothing more than abstractions—"imagined communities," to use Benedict Anderson's famous phrase—that have no independent reality over and above the reality of those human individuals who compose them.[10] It is this thought that leads George Kateb to write that patriotism:

> . . . is a readiness to die and to kill for an abstraction: nothing you can see all of, or feel as you feel the presence of another person, or comprehend. Patriotism, then, is a readiness to die and to kill for what is largely a figment of the imagination.[11]

Differences between nations, moreover, are frequently exaggerated in order to justify war, or to assuage our consciences about the acts performed in war. "There was no reason for the war in Bosnia," Chris Hedges has written. "The warring sides invented national myths and histories designed to mask the fact that Croats, Muslims, and Serbs are ethnically and linguistically indistinguishable."[12] A large part of the work of motivating human beings to engage in war involves just such inventions, for it is such inventions that make killing possible and, in the eyes of those who carry it out, justifiable.

PATRIOTISM AND DEHUMANIZATION

Understanding the evolutionary origins of loyalty and the ways in which these biologically instilled traits can be manipulated and exploited by countries, nations, institutions, and other actors takes us some distance toward understanding loyalty's double nature, the fact that it seems sometimes to be a virtue and other times to be a vice (or that it is a virtue that sometimes behaves like a vice). From a certain vantage point, loyalty is one of the greatest human goods, and it is hard to imagine living a fully flourishing life without it. But the very psychological facts that make loyalty so valuable and admirable also make human beings susceptible to certain forms of damaging and, at times, atrocious behavior. Appeals to tribal attachments, and the fears, hatreds, and stereotypes that they engender, are among the most powerful of factors that have inspired human beings to pick up guns or machetes and carry them to the places where the killing was done—the battlefields, the public squares, even the private homes of the victims.

Some have celebrated this aspect of loyalty, and have praised war in the name of loyalty. Josiah Royce describes (with commendable distaste) the German thinker Rudolf Steinmetz's view that "war gives an opportunity for loyal devotion so notable and important that, if war were altogether abolished, one of the greatest goods of civilization would thereby be hopelessly lost."[13] The "St Crispin's Day" speech in Shakespeare's HenryV makes beautiful rhetoric of these themes, mocking those who are cowardly enough to fear death, then going on to praise the bonds of loyalty and fellowship that are forged in battle:

> Rather proclaim it, Westmoreland, through my host,
> That he which hath no stomach to this fight,
> Let him depart; his passport shall be made,
> And crowns for convoy put into his purse;
> We would not die in that man's company
> That fears his fellowship to die with us.
>
> . . .
>
> We few, we happy few, we band of brothers;
> For he to-day that sheds his blood with me
> Shall be my brother; be he ne'er so vile . . . .

Such rhetoric can be moving, particularly when delivered by a skilled speaker, and indeed such orations have moved many human beings to acts of horrific violence. From a more critical standpoint, such appeals to heroic virtue will be found wanting in a couple of ways. First, they tend to ignore and efface the quite crucial issue of whether one is being called on to fight for the right side: rather, the fact that I am fighting for (and killing on behalf of) my side is taken to be enough of a justification, and larger questions about the morality of what one is doing are left to one side altogether. ("Ours is not to reason why," as Tennyson writes in "Charge of the Light Brigade.")

Second, such rhetoric tends to romanticize the character of war, deliberately and systematically obscuring the grim realities of the battlefield. Consider Rupert Brooke's poem "The Soldier":

> If I should die, think only this of me:
> That there's some corner of a foreign field
> That is for ever England. There shall be
> In that rich earth a richer dust concealed;
> A dust whom England bore, shaped, made aware,
> Gave, once, her flowers to love, her ways to roam,
> A body of England's, breathing English air,
> Washed by the rivers, blest by suns of home.
> And think, this heart, all evil shed away,
> A pulse in the eternal mind, no less
> Gives somewhere back the thoughts by England given;
> Her sights and sounds; dreams happy as her day;
> And laughter, learnt of friends; and gentleness,
> In hearts at peace, under an English heaven.[14]

A lovely scene to be sure; but the bucolic serenity depicted here has nothing whatever to do with the reality of the battlefield, or of the violent death the poem alludes to but avoids in any way describing. One would do better, if one wanted to learn about war and killing, to read Wilfred Owen's "*Dulce et Decorum Est*," with its powerful and disturbing account of a death by mustard gas. Here is the final stanza:

> If in some smothering dreams you too could pace
> Behind the wagon that we flung him in,
> And watch the white eyes writhing in his face,
> His hanging face, like a devil's sick of sin;
> If you could hear, at every jolt, the blood
> Come gargling from the froth-corrupted lungs,
> Obscene as cancer, bitter as the cud
> Of vile, incurable sores on innocent tongues,–
> My friend, you would not tell with such high zest
> To children ardent for some desperate glory,
> The old Lie: *Dulce et decorum est*
> *Pro patria mori.*[15]

One might also consult Randall Jarrell's "Death of the Ball Turret Gunner," with its unforgettable last line ("When I died they washed me out of the turret with a hose."[16]) As such works testify, the reality of war is neither beautiful nor romantic. If occasionally heroic, it is far more often ugly, grim, and vicious.

It cannot be denied that war does offer occasional opportunities for acts of courage and heroism. So do natural disasters, plagues, and other catastrophes. But to regard such events as justified, let alone desirable and praiseworthy, by the good human qualities whose display they occasionally allow is to sadly and callously discount the human misery suffered by the victims. (Imagine regarding the September 11 attacks as justified by the fact that they gave New York City firefighters the chance to display their valor.) It is to ignore something else, too, which is that in addition to allowing for the display of noble qualities, war also allows and, indeed, encourages those who take part to indulge and display the very worst aspects of their character. We might think again of the "honorable" obedience of members of the SS, or of the My Lai massacre, which at least some of the perpetrators themselves saw as displaying precisely the sort of "loyal devotion" Steinmetz had in mind.

Atrocities such as the Holocaust and My Lai happen in part because those who carry them out prize loyalty and obedience above thought and conscience, and in part due to the deep tribal instincts that, as we have seen, form much of the foundation of loyalty—instincts that sometimes make it easier for us to feel emotionally attached to an abstract, largely imagined entity such as a country or a nation than to a real human individual in all his concrete individuality. Part of tribalism, after all, is that one regards outsiders to one's tribe as less significant, less morally worthy, and often as less human than members of one's own tribe. "One million Arabs are not worth a Jewish fingernail," claimed the Rabbi Yaacov Perrin at the funeral of Baruch Goldstein, the perpetrator of the 1994 Cave of the Patriarchs massacre. The remark surely strikes us as revolting, but a related if substantially less extreme attitude is common in most nations, reflected in the news coverage offered by the mass media: an airplane crash in Africa will not be heavily covered in the U.S. unless there are Americans aboard, and if there are, then the number of Americans killed will be the story's leading detail. The process of dividing humanity into "us" and "them" is sometimes more overt, sometimes less so, and can be all the more insidious for being less so; but while its manifestation and expression can take various forms, it is a candidate for being a genuinely universal aspect of human affairs.

This fact about human nature provides a useful tool for political and military leaders who need somehow to overcome the natural revulsion that ordinary human beings feel toward the act of killing other human beings. The grimmest and least romantic aspect of the reality of war, and the one that the rhetoric of militaristic patriotism must work hardest to obscure, is the fact that the person on the receiving end of the deadly violence one inflicts is, indeed, a *person*—a human being with a human face, a human mind, and a very human capacity to suffer. "Close combat," as Jonathan Glover writes, "also requires the overcoming of the moral resources. Combatants need to escape the inhibitions of human responses: of respect and sympathy for others. They need to escape the restraints of moral identity: of their sense of not being a person who would wound and kill."[17] Not an easy task, but thanks to our tribal tendencies, the means are available: by playing on our deep-rooted tribal tensions, and by amplifying perceptions of members of other communities as outsiders (to one's own community, and perhaps to the human community at large), it is often possible to bring ordinary people to a point where they are not only willing to kill but will think little of it.

We have already noted that it is essential to get potential killers to see their victims as non-relatives, as excluded from the tribe. Even more powerful is to blind them to the humanity or individuality of their victims. Being perceived as an individual—even as an unrelated individual—encourages the recognition of human commonality: it reminds one that the person before one is, like oneself, an emotional and intellectual being, a person with an identity, thoughts, and desires of his own, and a creature with a physical presence in the world that can suffer, and whose suffering is awful. To do evil to others, then, it is frequently necessary to see them as something other than human individuals: not true individuals, and perhaps not truly human. Consider what is perhaps the most famous scene from The Third Man. Harry Lime and Holly Martins are atop a Ferris wheel in Vienna, and when Martins asks Lime if he has ever seen any of his victims, Lime responds as follows:

> Victims? Don't be melodramatic. Look down there. Tell me. Would you really feel any pity if one of those dots stopped moving forever? If I offered you twenty thousand pounds for every dot that stopped, would you really, old man, tell me to keep my money, or would you calculate how many dots you could afford to spare? Free of income tax, old man. Free of income tax—the only way you can save money nowadays.

The most effective way of dehumanizing others in order to immunize yourself from the effects your actions have on them is often to view them collectively rather than as distinct individuals. After all, it often is not possible literally to see other human beings as tiny dots. (Admittedly, and unfortunately, remote-controlled drones and other contemporary military technologies are making that possibility ever more real in the context of war.) Instead, we use other techniques—using racial stereotyping, for instance, to make them seem less like humans and more like animals, or else reducing all of the individuals on "the other side" to a collective ideology or collective threat. William Calley, the commanding officer at My Lai, testified that:

> I was ordered to go in there and destroy the enemy. That was my job on that day. That was the mission I was given. I did not sit down and think in terms of men, women and children. They were all classified the same, and that was the classification that we dealt with, just as enemy soldiers . . . When my troops were getting massacred and mauled by an enemy I couldn't see, I couldn't feel and I couldn't touch, nobody in the military system ever described them as anything other than Communism. They didn't give it a race, they didn't give it a sex, they didn't give it an age.[18]

The idea of shooting at "the enemy" or at "Communism" seems somehow far less objectionable than the idea of shooting a *person*. This interplay of loyalty and collectivization or dehumanization is as complex as it is deadly. The victim of one's deadly action is objectified as "the enemy." His status as the enemy may be due, in part, to the fact that he is loyal to his cause, which is opposed to one's own. His loyalty, then, renders him collectively responsible for the badness of the other side. (As mentioned earlier, this "badness" might not reflect a judgment that the other side is *objectively* evil or bad—for many, the fact that the other side is the *other* side, and thus opposed to one's own, is enough to render them automatically bad.) But in other cases "enemy" status may be conferred on the basis of mere membership in a political, national, or cultural group. For Horace Bottomley, all German-born individuals—even those who were citizens of the United Kingdom—were contaminated by their German identity and were thus untrustworthy and morally loathsome. After Pearl Harbor, U.S. citizens of Japanese ancestry were regarded as inherently untrustworthy, again by virtue of their ethnicity alone.

One's reaction to *one's own* memberships, and one's own loyalty to the "right" side, is taken to mean something quite different: these facts about oneself are interpreted both as providing a moral justification for one's violent behavior (since it is done in the name of all that is good and holy) and, where such behavior might be somewhat morally questionable, as rendering one *less* responsible for those actions. The U.S. army's *Soldier's Guide* tells recruits that "Enlisted soldiers also promise to obey the orders of the President and the officers appointed over them. Every team has a leader, and that leader is responsible for what the team does or fails to do. That is why obeying orders is necessary; your leader is responsible for all your military actions."[19] We are reminded, again, of the Colin Powell understanding of loyalty that sees it as involving the willingness to carry out another person's decision "as if it were your own." The logical conclusion of this is that one's membership in and loyalty to one's community are taken to render one less responsible—one is only carrying out the will of the collective, after all—while the affiliations and loyalties of those one is trying to kill cause him to be absorbed into a collective in a way that renders them responsible for the larger group's crimes, and thus renders them, like the collective itself, worthy of annihilation.

MORAL DANGER AND IMPERSONAL LOYALTIES

My general focus in this chapter has been on loyalties such as patriotism, nationalism, and their ilk—the sort of loyalties that are directed toward larger political, social, or corporate entities rather than toward specific persons, and which tend to play such an important role in motivating war, terrorism, and other forms of impersonal violence. I would not assert, though, that personal loyalties are never bad: as we have already observed, loyalty to friends, lovers, or family members can tempt us toward dishonesty, injustice, and other regrettable behaviors. Nor do I mean to make the claim that the more impersonal loyalties are always bad. We must allow that some degree of loyalty is probably necessary to the survival of any community, and there are occasions on which loyalty to state or country can motivate people to act better than they would if they were moved only by self-interested rational calculation.

Still, the tensions here are real and deep. On the one hand, we need people to hold to a certain level of loyalty or obedience in order to make any large institution work. One must be willing to wait to confirm that the ship really is sinking before heading for the life rafts. Yet it is also true that people need sometimes to disobey orders, to listen to their conscience and allow themselves to reach the conclusion that the society or institution they have been loyal to no longer deserves that loyalty. The United States, to take the country where I have lived for some decades now, would be considerably better off if more people had been willing to disobey orders to shoot the civilians at My Lai, and even try to save them; to refuse to take part in the abuse of prisoners at Abu Ghraib, and to bring those abuses before the public; or to point out that the best available intelligence never supported the hypothesis that Iraq possessed weapons of mass destruction in 2001/2002.

In general, we have more reason to worry about larger, impersonal loyalties—the sort of loyalties I have tended to focus more attention on in this book—than about personal loyalties directed toward human individuals. This is a general claim, not a universal one, and is meant to allow for exceptions. It is meant to allow, for instance, that larger, more impersonal loyalties, including loyalties to one's country, one's nation, and one's religious faith, can sometimes move us to perform good, valuable, even admirable actions. Conversely, personal, professional, and other local loyalties can move us to act in ways that range from the morally questionable ("A Father's Story") to the clearly reprehensible (*The Remains of the Day*).

Nonetheless, as a generalization it seems to me that the claim is true. Impersonal, "larger" loyalties are on the whole more morally dangerous and less morally justifiable than "smaller," personal loyalties. This is partly because of differences in the inherent natures of the various objects: as I have suggested earlier, individual persons are appropriate objects of loyalties in various ways in which societies and large institutions are not. Human individuals need and deserve special attention, and are vulnerable to experiencing pain and suffering when betrayed. Countries, nations, large corporations, and other such entities cannot experience anything and do not morally deserve anything in the literal sense in which human beings do.

But the difference is not only grounded in whether the objection in question is a suitable object of loyalty. It is also due, in part, to differences in the typical consequences of extending our loyalties in these ways. Being loyal to an individual leads one to treat that particular person as an individual, while at the same time reminding us of the value of human individuals in general; whereas being loyal to one's tribe, country, or nation, or to any other abstraction, often encourages one to efface and suppress the particularity of others. This is particularly true in times of conflict—and as Kateb observes, the state of conflict is the natural state that exists between nations and states. "You can love particular persons without having to dislike or hate others," he writes, "but you cannot love an abstract entity like a country and not dislike or hate other countries, because countries are, from their nature as organizations of and for power, in actual or latent competition."[20] Loyalties directed toward human individuals tend to counteract, rather than reinforce, our inherent tendency to ignore the unique individuality of others. And it is partly because of this that, while loyalties to individual persons have an inherent tendency to make people better versions of themselves, loyalties to political and corporate entities seem more commonly to make people behave worse than they otherwise would.

Four

LOYALTY, IMPARTIALITY, AND MORALITY

Until recently, modern moral philosophers tended to assume that morality must be fundamentally impartial, and that treating all persons without favoritism or partiality was the essence of acting morally. Such a view seems to leave little room for loyalty as a moral phenomenon. Loyalty is necessarily partial: the idea of being loyal to *everyone* makes nonsense of the concept. And given the ways in which our loyalties can encourage conflict, intolerance, and violence, it is understandable that some would suggest that we ought to resist the temptations of loyalty.

Others have taken an opposing view, insisting that loyalty has been under-appreciated in modern times, and that to attempt to leave any form of it behind is to move in precisely the wrong direction. What we need, these thinkers suggest, is not fewer and weaker particularistic commitments, but more and stronger ones. Some of these philosophers have called themselves *communitarians*. The term is hard to define precisely, but for our purposes we can see communitarians as being united by the claims that community identity is more important, morally speaking, than universalistic philosophers have realized; that this importance reflects the fact that morality is *not* universalistic, but rather grounded in community; and that loyalty to one's community is not only morally virtuous, but quite possibly a prerequisite for being moral in any substantial sense at all.

The idea that loyalty somehow grounds morality is perhaps the main idea of Josiah Royce's *The Philosophy of Loyalty*—a book that appeared in 1908 and thus predates "communitarianism" as a movement by a number of decades. "There is only one way to be an ethical individual," Royce writes, and "that is to choose your cause, and then to serve it, as the Samurai his feudal chief, as the ideal knight of romantic story his lady,— in the spirit of the Loyal."[1] More recent thinkers have picked up this theme. "All morality is tribal morality," writes Andrew Oldenquist.[2] And as Alasdair MacIntyre writes: "Loyalty to [one's] community, to the hierarchy of particular kinship, particular local community, and particular natural community, is . . . a prerequisite for morality."[3]

Why think that loyalty, far from being a potentially if not inherently immoral force, is in fact a presupposition of morality? Communitarians tend to emphasize that community membership is a deep constituent of personal identity, and to claim that something important about the justification or nature of morality follows from this. Michael Sandel, for instance, contrasts his communitarian view with a liberal or "deontological" view of human morality, which sees human individuals as isolated agents choosing freely from among a range of values. In his influential book *Liberalism and the Limits of Justice*, he writes that:

> . . . we cannot regard ourselves as independent in this way without great cost to those loyalties and convictions whose moral force consists partly in the fact that living by them is inseparable from understanding ourselves as the particular persons we are – as members of this family or community

or nation or people, as bearers of this history, as sons and daughters of that revolution, as citizens of this republic . . . To imagine a person incapable of constitutive attachments such as these is not to conceive an ethically free and rational agent, but to imagine a person wholly without character, without moral depth. For to have character is to know that I move in a history I neither summon nor command, which carries consequences none the less for my choices and conduct. It draws me closer to some and more distant from others; it makes some aims more appropriate, others less so. A person with character thus knows that he is implicated in various ways even as he reflects, and feels the moral weight of what he knows.[4]

In one way this might sound reminiscent of some of the claims I have made about moral dilemmas. In urging that we should allow that a person might, as a result of conflicting loyalties, be placed in a dilemma that she could not have chosen to avoid, I am in essence acknowledging the reality of "a history I neither summon nor command, which carries consequences nonetheless for my choices and conduct." We should not assume too quickly, though, that a person who accepts that view of loyalty conflicts must accept every part of the kind of view that Sandel has in mind. I have not, after all, made any particular claims about which particular loyalties apply to an agent. I have only said that some of those loyalties might attach to us without our voluntarily choosing that they do so. This, I take it, leaves it entirely open whether one must agree with Sandel, MacIntyre, and other communitarians that in order to be moral one must be loyal to one's community, particularly where this is understood as including the requirement that one accept, at the fundamental level, that community's moral standards and views.

"AN EARTH THAT HAD NO MAPS": COSMOPOLITANISM IN *THE ENGLISH PATIENT*

Michael Ondaatje's 1992 novel *The English Patient* takes place at the tail end of the Second World War, and begins with Hana, a Canadian nurse who has chosen to remain behind in an unsafe Italian villa when the rest of the division to which she was attached has moved on, in order to care for the "English patient" of the title. Hana, Ondaatje writes, "would not be ordered again or carry out duties for the greater good. She would care only for the burned patient. She would read to him and bathe him and give him his doses of morphine— her only communication was with him."[5] Hana's skepticism about "the greater good" and her decision to devote herself to the care of a single individual show that she has, at least for herself, answered the question we found Sartre asking in the context of moral dilemmas: "Which is the more useful aim—the vague one of fighting as part of a group, or the more concrete one of helping one particular person keep on living?"

The English patient himself is both a symbol and a mystery. As it turns out, he is a Hungarian count named László de Almásy. But Almásy is, in his own way, a man without a country, identifying more strongly with the aristocratic class from which he emerged than he does with any particular country or ethnicity. The terrible burns that cover most of his body and have effectively erased his identity serve, in the novel, as a metaphor for his reluctance to identify himself by means of traditional signs. "The burned pilot was one more enigma, with no identification, unrecognizable" (p95). As a cosmopolitan, a kind of cultural pluralist, he is deeply curious about human cultural and intellectual achievements regardless of their origin, and bears the identifying marks of a large number of countries and cultures:

"You should be trying to trick me," the burned pilot told his interrogators, "make me speak German, which I can, by the way, ask me about Don Bradman. Ask me about Marmite, the great Gertrude Jekyll." He knew where every Giotto was in Europe, and most of the places where a person could find convincing trompe l'oeil. (p95)

For the cosmopolitan individual who considers himself a cultural world citizen and who therefore exists between and draws from multiple countries, to speak German is not to be German, any more than to eat Marmite is to be English. And to accept any of these national identities as defining oneself runs counter to the deep pluralism of the cosmopolitan spirit, which would have us take pleasure in all the cultural achievements of the human race, regardless of the particular culture in which they might have originated. "I wanted to erase my name and the place I had come from," says Almásy, commenting later that "We are communal histories, communal books. We are not owned or monogamous in our taste or experience. All I desired was to walk upon such an earth that had no maps" (pp139, 261).

Almásy, at any rate, is used to being surrounded with people who are not "owned or monogamous in [their] taste or experience": the coterie of aristocrats—desert explorers, mostly—who used to constitute his personal community came from a diverse group of European countries and saw themselves as standing above and apart from their particular countries. "We were German, English, Hungarian, African— all of us insignificant to them," he states. "Gradually we became nationless. I came to hate nations. We are deformed by nation-states" (p138). The prime deformity is that of war, the organized slaughter of citizens of one country by citizens of another. As Almásy says of his friend Madox, who has committed suicide:

> Someone's war was slashing apart his delicate tapestry
> of companions. I was Odysseus, I understood the shifting
> and temporary vetoes of war. But he was a man who made
> friends with difficulty. He was a man who knew two or three
> people in his life, and they had turned out now to be the
> enemy. (p241)

Almásy, then, represents a cosmopolitan rejection of the particularistic nationalistic sentiments and attachments that lay behind many if not most of the wars of the twentieth century. His stance is deeply opposed to the division of the globe into multiple sovereign states—states that tend to promote, encourage, and reify such local loyalties and obligations, and that tend to come into conflict, frequently armed and sometimes devastating conflict, with one another. He is not, on the other hand, opposed to loyalty *per se*; but his loyalties are to individuals, to Madox and his other friends, and particularly to his lover, Katherine Clifton.

The English Patient's stance toward this cosmopolitanism is complex. We are clearly meant to feel that there is something attractive and admirable about it.[6] But Almásy's full story, which only gradually emerges, makes the reader unable to wholeheartedly approve. For what we eventually discover is that out of loyalty to Katherine—who was injured in the desert and, it turns out, was dead before the main action of the novel began—Almásy performed a valuable service for the Germans: he guided a pair of Nazi spies across the desert to Cairo. And it was, it seems, precisely his cosmopolitanism that blinded him to the moral seriousness of this act. "There are betrayals in war that are childlike compared with our human betrayals during peace," he has written in his journal, indicating that in his view, war and other affairs of nations are not only "childlike," they are not even fully *human* (p97). And it is this refusal to take sides, this idealistic insistence on treating nations and their concerns as trivial and childish matters, that renders him unable to perceive that the Second World War, for all its politics, cannot simply be written off as a stupid conflagration of belligerent nations. In this case, at least, it actually mattered that one side rather than the other emerge victorious.

HOW MIGHT MORALITY DEPEND ON COMMUNITY?

We need to pause here for some clarification, both of terms and of concepts. The word "cosmopolitan," which I have used to describe Almásy, has a special meaning in the context of debates about communitarianism. Like "communitarianism," "cosmopolitanism" is difficult to define precisely in a way that everyone will accept. But those who take up the anti-communitarian side of the so-called cosmopolitan–communitarian debate typically build their views around the following claims:[7]

1 Every human individual has equal moral standing.
2 All human beings are similar to each other in fundamental ways that tend to be obscured by the misguided emphasis placed by many (in particular, by communitarians) on cultural or national differences.
3 The identity of each person as a "citizen of the world" (or as a member of the human race) is more fundamental than her identity as a citizen of some particular state.
4 The structure of our moral duties should reflect 1, 2, and 3. (Most immediately, our duties to those who live far

from us, or under other political regimes, should not be less stringent than our duties to our neighbors.)

5 All human beings should be members of the same state, living under one government whose authority extends over the entire globe. For the most part, the commitment to the existence of a global state is instrumental: the idea is that establishing such a state is the best way of recognizing and protecting the moral rights and claims that would have to be recognized if 1 through 4 were true.

Of these claims, the second and the fifth seem most central to Almásy's outlook, and it is his commitment to the second (his skepticism about the significance of national differences) that leads him to a version of the fifth (his antipathy toward the existence of borders between states). His commitment to the other elements of the cosmopolitan outlook is less clear. In principle, he most likely accepts that all human beings have equal moral standing in some fundamental sense; at any rate, he almost certainly thinks that their citizenship or national identity is irrelevant to the question of what sort of moral standing they have. But there is no evidence that he is committed to this as a kind of political program, as contemporary cosmopolitans such as Martha Nussbaum would urge us to be. And, indeed, the same can be said of his stance toward the fifth claim: his hatred of borders is not shown in any kind of campaign to eliminate them—rather, he simply wishes that they were not there, and thus tends to treat them with disdain. It is entirely possible that he would be completely satisfied by a world in which *he* could simply ignore borders between countries—a world in which such inconvenient historical events as the Second World War did not create difficulties for his pursuit of his personal projects and interests—whether or not the rest of the world's inhabitants were granted a similar privilege.

A communitarian might well suggest that the kind of self-involved elitism we see in Almásy is the natural end product of the cosmopolitan viewpoint.[8] The argument for this claim might be that since it is impossible for an individual to literally care about everyone in the world, people will tend to care only about those who are part of their social group; but this means that we need a way of defining who is in our social group and distinguishing them from those who are not—a task that the cosmopolitan resistance to social divisions would render impossible. Thus, the cosmopolitan, who begins by expressing the desire to be concerned for all human beings, will end up being concerned only about those with whom he has direct personal relations—a much smaller number than he might have been concerned with had he accepted the sorts of loyalties communitarians think we ought to recognize.

Most communitarians, though, seem to have something much stronger than motivational dependence in mind when they argue that morality depends in some way on one's community. Consider the following version of the argument offered by Alasdair MacIntyre:

> *If* first of all it is the case that I can only apprehend the rules of morality in the version in which they are incarnated in some specific community; and *if* secondly it is the case that the justification of morality must be in terms of particular goods enjoyed within the life of particular communities; and *if* thirdly it is the case that I am characteristically brought into being and maintained as a moral agent only through the particular kinds of sustenance afforded by my moral community, *then* it is clear that deprived of this community,

I am unlikely to flourish as a moral agent. Hence my allegiance to the community and what it requires of me—even to the point of requiring me to die to sustain its life—could not meaningfully be contrasted with or counterposed to what morality required of me. Detached from my community, I will be liable to lose my hold upon all genuine standards of judgment. Loyalty to that community, to the hierarchy of particular kinship, particular local community, and particular natural community, is on this view a prerequisite for morality. So patriotism and those loyalties cognate to it are not just virtues but central virtues.[9]

Just what is the argument here supposed to be? The remark that "I am characteristically brought into being and maintained as a moral agent only through the particular kinds of sustenance afforded by my moral community" seems to suggest that what is at issue is a kind of *causal* dependence: I literally would not exist as a moral agent if it were not for my community. This is true, of course, but it seems trivial; it is equally true that a mathematician would not exist as a mathematician if not for her community—without social support she would not have existed at all, and she presumably acquired her knowledge of mathematics from others—but the dependence of mathematicians on the existence of a community does not imply that mathematical *facts*, say, are community dependent in any interesting way. Similarly, the fact that the budding moral agent must learn morality in some particular form does not seem to imply that she must therefore accept that particular form or agree with her society's valuing of particular goods.

Perhaps what MacIntyre wants to suggest is that given the community's role in creating and nurturing me, I owe it a kind of loyalty and a kind of obedience. This account, which points to a kind of normative dependence, is perhaps suggested by the remark that "deprived of this community, I am unlikely to flourish as a moral agent. Hence my allegiance to the community and what it requires of me ... could not meaningfully be contrasted with or counterposed to what morality required of me." But this rests on a controversial theory of normative reasons, and one we almost certainly should reject. After all, if my community is deeply evil (suppose it has engaged in longstanding and consistent persecution of weaker neighboring communities, in the process of which it has committed, and celebrated, genuinely atrocious human rights violations), then the fact that that community gave me life and support, and thus enabled my flourishing, hardly obligates me to obey or serve it. It might obligate me to start refusing its support, even at the cost of my own flourishing; but that is a separate question.

Another possibility is that morality would be indeterminate, or empty of content, without the authority of the community to be the final arbiter of moral disputes. Perhaps this is what MacIntyre means when he suggests that "the justification of morality must be in terms of particular goods enjoyed within the life of particular communities." The point is that there are no universal goods that can serve to ground morality, only particular goods that have been selected by communities in a way that is not entirely arbitrary (one hopes) but cannot be justified in terms of an overarching universal hierarchy either.

This version of the argument is motivated by a kind of skepticism about values: the decisions of the community are, in this view, needed to establish the truth of claims about value precisely because there are no objectively established facts about what is good and what is bad. If there are no independent and objectively true value claims—as communitarians of this stripe typically assume is the case—what could plug the gap *other than* the evaluative standards of our particular communities? In the absence of generally shared community standards, either there would be no standards at all, or any standards we might come up with and try to establish for ourselves (as existentialists, for instance, will suggest that we do) must be fundamentally arbitrary.

This, at any rate, is the way in which I read the following passage from Sandel's *Liberalism and the Limits of Justice*:

> . . . the deontological self, being wholly without character, is incapable of self-knowledge in any morally serious sense. Where the self is unencumbered and essentially dispossessed, no person is left for *self*-reflection to reflect upon. That is why, on the deontological view, deliberation about ends can only be an exercise in arbitrariness. In the absence of constitutive attachments, deliberation issues in "purely preferential choice," which means the ends we seek, being mired in contingency, "are not relevant from a moral standpoint." (Rawls 1975: 537).
>
> When I act out of more or less enduring qualities of character, by contrast, my choice of ends is not arbitrary in the same way. In consulting my preferences, I have not only to weigh their intensity but also to assess their suitability to the person I (already) am. I ask, as I deliberate, not only what I really want but who I really am, and this last question takes me beyond an attention to my desires alone to reflect on my identity itself . . . Although there may be a certain ultimate contingency in my having wound up the person I am—only theology can say for sure—it makes a moral difference none the less that, being the person I am, I affirm these ends

> rather than those, turn this way rather than that. While the notion of constitutive attachments may at first seem an obstacle to agency—the self, now encumbered, is no longer strictly prior—some relative fixity of character appears essential to prevent the lapse into arbitrariness which the [unencumbered] self is unable to avoid.[10]

One thing that is not immediately apparent is why Sandel thinks we are entitled to assume that deliberation about ends must take the form of *self*-reflection—that is, that questions about what ends one should adopt must be settled by facts about one's own commitments and relationships. To think this, I have suggested, one must presumably think that there are no objective values that could answer such questions—or, at any rate, that the objective values that do exist do not fully determine the answers. But then why should historical facts about oneself, as opposed to facts about what one desires, etc., be any more authoritative? Sandel points out that desires are largely contingent, but whether this is so depends on one's theory of desire; but more pressing is the point that facts about one's history—the family and community whom one has been born into and brought up in—are themselves just as contingent. (Sandel's casual dismissal of the fact that there not only "may be" but surely is "a certain ultimate contingency in my having wound up the person I am" is telling, and his insistence that "it makes a moral difference none the less that, being the person I am, I affirm these ends rather than those, turn this way rather than that" is question-begging. Why not insist that it makes a moral difference whether I try to satisfy my own desires or to frustrate or alter them?) Community values might have the feeling of objectivity in that they are not entirely up to us; but the feeling of objectivity is not objectivity, and as it is, after all, up to us whether to endorse or reject such values, no real progress toward genuine objectivity is made by treating such facts as authoritative on the level of theory.

Related to this is that it is very difficult, if not impossible, to keep communitarianism from reducing to a form of relativism. If the individual cannot transcend the moral views of her community—if even her critiques of those views must ultimately fall back on standards of rationality and justification that are defined by that very community—then it seems to follow that *any* sort of moral view, no matter how outrageous, will be justifiable and, indeed, obligatory should one happen to grow up within the conceptual confines of a community who accepts it. To hold this is to abandon the idea that morality is objective or universal in any meaningful sense, and thus to render morality both arbitrary and fundamentally dangerous. As Anna Stilz has put the point, saying that one has political obligations to one's *polis* simply because one's own identity is deeply entangled with it "is like saying that someone who is born a member of the Mafia has unchosen obligations to his fellow members, simply because he has grown up in the group and it has come to play a significant role in his own conception of himself."[11]

COSMOPOLITANISM AND MOTIVATION

This seems to leave only the motivational issue: the worry that, given the difficulty of choosing consistently to be moral and of resisting the temptations to immorality that the world constantly presents us with, a moral agent needs to draw on the resources of her community in order to be motivated to act well. It seems unlikely that this is all that MacIntyre had in mind, since the argument, interpreted this way, could hardly establish the conclusion that "my allegiance to the community and what it requires of me—even to the point of requiring me to die to sustain its life—[cannot] meaningfully be contrasted with or counterposed to what morality required of me." It seems unable, too, to support the claim that "detached from my community, I will be liable to lose my hold upon all genuine standards of judgment"—unless, of course, the "hold" in question refers only to one's *motivational* grip.

Nonetheless, interpreting the dependence argument in terms of motivation might be the communitarian's best and, perhaps, only hope of making the argument work. Suppose we start with the claim that Almásy's problem is that he simply does not care enough about what happens to people who fall outside the small circle of his friends and relatives. We might then think that the best strategy for reformulating the anti-cosmopolitan argument would be to take the conclusion of the argument to be something like this:

> Detached from my community, I will be liable to *stop caring about* genuine standards of judgment.

If this is the conclusion, what are the premises? The worry is that the kind of lack of empathy and narrowed moral vision that Almásy represents might be a necessary or predictable result of a cosmopolitan commitment to equal recognition of everyone's moral standing. If so, then making cosmopolitan commitments is a bad moral practice, and the commitments themselves are self-defeating. A natural thought might hold this to be so due to human psychological limitations. Given the limits of human capacities for caring, trying to care about everyone is bound to fail, and the inevitable result, it might be claimed, will be that one will constrict one's empathy to a small circle of acquaintances.

How convincing should we find this argument? If we insist on interpreting it along standard communitarian lines—as emphasizing the agent's reliance on the community who formed her as a moral agent, and thus her inability to achieve any sort of substantial independence from that community—it turns out not to be exceptionally convincing. To begin, we can note that it is not completely clear that in Almásy's case, his self-involvement is the *effect* of his cosmopolitan sentiments. What appears to be the case, rather, is that Almásy was not at any point in time enthusiastically committed to the cosmopolitan program of moral equality for all. He is more profoundly moved by the idea that focusing on national characteristics tends to impede our ability to relate to human beings as individuals, and while this is, indeed, a cosmopolitan sentiment, it does not take one all the way to the sort of moral cosmopolitanism espoused by, say, Diogenes in ancient times or by Martha Nussbaum in ours. Indeed, one can be opposed to nationalism in just this way while having no moral concern whatsoever for anyone outside of the circle of one's own friends and loved ones. In fact, one might actually be opposed to attempts to take a more global perspective precisely on the basis that doing so would constrict or interfere with our relations to those closest to us.

There seems to be no reason, then, to assume that every aspiring cosmopolitan must end up as Almásy does. Indeed, there are real-world cases that strongly suggest the opposite. The Australian philosopher Peter Singer, for instance, has spent several decades arguing for a version of moral cosmopolitanism, and this does not seem to have diminished his motivation either for continuing to press the argument or for attempting to embody cosmopolitan ideals in his own life—by, for example, donating a substantial fraction of his income to charity.[12] We should immediately acknowledge that Singer himself admits that he does not give *as much* to charity as his moral view implies he should, and this might signal that there are, indeed, certain psychological boundaries that will limit even the most committed moral universalist. What it does not suggest, though, is that Singer would be a better person if he were to eschew his commitment to cosmopolitanism. Singer may fall somewhat short of his very demanding ideal, but he still comes much closer than most of us to meeting its demands.

Critics of cosmopolitanism are correct to claim that it is not possible literally to care about every existing human being to an equal degree, or indeed to care about every human being at all. But to conclude from this that cosmopolitanism is therefore pointless if not morally hazardous is to confuse what we feel with how we choose to act. A reasonable cosmopolitan will acknowledge that one cannot literally feel empathy for every human being, given how many of them there are. But what matters, she will remind us, is whether one *acts* in a way that recognizes the fundamental humanity and equal moral standing of all people. And one need not actually feel empathy for everyone in order to do this: human beings are capable of choosing to adopt policies and modes of behavior that they consistently adhere to even on those occasions where their ordinary emotional resources are, for whatever reason, not available. Or to put the point more colloquially, sometimes it's possible to be a good person, even when you don't feel like it.

This is so, at any rate, so long as we take the crucial issue to be that of whether moral agents are able to achieve substantial independence from the moral communities that formed them. This, again, is the issue that many communitarians are inclined to take as crucial. And these communitarians get little help from examples such as Singer, whose moral view is both radical and critical of the prevailing views of the society in which he was raised, views which place far more importance on local interests and parochial concerns than does Singer's ethical theory.

Here, the communitarian might make a last-ditch effort to save her position, claiming that the roots of Singer's ethical view are nonetheless present, if buried, in the views of the community who raised and formed Singer. Nearly every contemporary moral view, after all, pays at least lip service to the universalist claim that all human beings are worthy of equal consideration. But in making this move, the communitarian risks making her position trivial: if Singer's view is going to count as an expression of the prevailing moral views of the society who formed him, then nearly any moral position is going to count. Moreover, to allow a position like Singer's, which refuses to grant any intrinsic significance whatsoever to particularistic loyalties (not only to states and nations, but to individuals as well) to count as a kind of communitarian morality is to sever the link between community, morality, and loyalty that was supposed to be so crucial in the communitarian view.

SOLIDARITY

Is this to say that community plays no role in the motivation of individuals? I don't think we need to go that far. We do, though, need to give up the idea that the community that matters is necessarily the one identified by the communitarian–that is, the one that formed the moral agent. Through decades of work, Peter Singer has managed to attract a large number of supporters and like-minded persons. Would he have continued to campaign on behalf of a radical morality if he had had to do so as an entirely isolated individual, without any sort of support from friends or fellow travelers? It is entirely possible that the answer is no: the fact is that such work is hard, and there will be times when the only thing that keeps such a person going is his knowledge that in his endeavor he is not, at any rate, alone.

To put the point in broader terms: the problem the cosmopolitan faces might be that any attempt to improve the global condition of mankind is, of necessity, a joint undertaking, and we cannot rely on humanity at large to share our purposes and support our efforts in the way that we can rely on those who are close to us, those whom we trust. Sartre seems to be making this point when he writes:

> I will always depend on my comrades-in-arms in the struggle, inasmuch as they are committed, as I am, to a definite common cause, in the solidarity of a party or a group that I can more or less control—that is to say, that I joined the group as a militant and so its every move is familiar to me. In that context, counting on the solidarity and will of this party is exactly like counting on the fact that the train will arrive on time, or that the trolley will not derail. But I cannot count on men whom I do not know based on faith in the goodness of humanity or in man's interest in society's welfare, given that man is free and there is no human nature in which I can place my trust. I do not know where the Russian Revolution might lead. I can admire it and hold it up as an example to the extent that it is clear, to date, that the proletariat plays a part in Russia that it has attained in no other nation. But I cannot assert that this revolution will necessarily lead to the triumph of the proletariat; I must confine myself to what I can see.[13]

At least some of our moral motivations, then, might well depend upon a type of loyalty—the loyalty we bear to those who share our moral projects, in particular those who are aiming to revise and re-invent the status quo. But if ours is a radical moral program that is critical of the society who raised us, then that society will not be the community upon whose motivational resources we draw. Rather, as with Singer and Sartre, the relevant supporting community will be an independent, largely self-selected network of like-minded moral reformers.

There is, then, a motivational issue, and one that might pose a special problem for the cosmopolitan in the sense that she, in adhering to and promoting a radical moral view, will be unable to rely on the support of her original moral community and will have to go looking elsewhere. But there is little reason to think that this problem is insurmountable—the existence of real-world cosmopolitans such as Peter Singer suggests otherwise; and at any rate, it is important to recall that this is, at most, a practical problem, not an issue of principle. The importance of the kind of solidarity that comes from being tied to fellow travelers through bonds of loyalty is very real, and to the extent that this is what the communitarian is emphasizing, we should agree with her. But we can do that without endorsing the bolder claims that tend to be characteristic of communitarianism: that universal morality has no content, that community values can serve as adequate substitutes for genuinely objective moral values and thus terminate otherwise interminable moral debates by fiat, or that the needs of one's community must necessarily coincide with the dictates of morality. In particular, the communitarian view that in order to be moral at all, an agent is required to be patriotic, or to display some other form of loyalty to the moral community who formed her, should be rejected. The ties between loyalty and morality are simply not that close.

Conclusion

If loyalty tends to be overvalued or overpraised, by communitarians and others, it is for two reasons. The first is the basic human tendency to fear being betrayed, the concomitant tendency to wonder whether any person whose views and behavior seem threatening or even merely odd is really "one of us," and the corresponding anxiety one feels at being so judged by others. (This is closely related to the basic human need for committed relationships with individuals on whom one can rely—a tendency which also leads us to value loyalty highly, but not, here, to overvalue it.) The second is that most human beings would not desire either to be, or to be acquainted with, a person who was incapable of loyalty. Indeed, the prospect of a person who genuinely possesses no loyalties at all—if we can even imagine such a person—is deeply terrifying.

No one who has seen Joel and Ethan Coen's 2006 cinematic adaptation of Cormac McCarthy's novel No Country for Old Men is likely to forget Javier Bardem's Academy Award-winning performance as the psychopathic killer Anton Chigurh. Chigurh terrifies both for what he is and for what he is not. He is intelligent, determined, resourceful, and utterly ruthless. He has a code of ethics, of a sort, and, though it is rarely seen, he seems to have a sense of humor. (We see it when he toys cruelly with the gas station owner who "married into" his sad little life.) What he does not seem to have is the slightest hint of empathy, or indeed any sort of emotional or sentimental attachment to another human being. It would not be fair to say that he has no conscience; as mentioned above, he abides by a certain code of ethics. It is important to him, for example, that he keeps his promises. But his conscience and ethics do not recognize the desires, interests, or needs of other people.

Does Anton Chigurh have friends? It is impossible to imagine that he does. One cannot picture him returning home to his wife and children at the end of his adventures, or meeting some buddies at the local pub to brag about his escapades. Indeed, several characters in the film, including Sheriff Ed Tom Bell (Tommy Lee Jones), comment on the fact that he barely exists at all. ("Sometimes I think he's pretty much a ghost," says Bell.) There is, moreover, a perplexing scene near the end of the film in which Ed Tom opens the door to a motel room where we believe Chigurh to be, only to find the room empty. Chigurh works hard to maintain this virtual non-existence; indeed, with only a couple of exceptions, everyone who actually sees him ends up dead. Chigurh has turned his back on every human connection, every social attachment, every possible membership in a human community. One would have to turn one's back on such things, perhaps, to be so effective a killer.

Aristotle says that a man with no country and no community would be either a beast or a god.[1] There is, indeed, an element of the divine in Anton Chigurh—a terrifying Old Testament-type of pitiless, wrathful divinity. And there is, without a doubt, something terribly beastly about him as well.

What makes *No Country for Old Men* a profound film, though, is not its picture of Chigurh, as compelling and memorable as that is, but the way it puts its two other main characters into the position of questioning their own allegiances to the larger communities that surround them. There is Sheriff Ed Tom Bell, the aging lawman who, feeling overwhelmed by the challenges he faces as a law enforcement officer, is steadily distancing himself from that role and contemplating the prospect of retiring altogether. And there is Llewellyn Moss (Josh Brolin), the fairly ordinary man who, as luck would have it, stumbles across the bag of money that Chigurh and others are pursuing.

Moss is alone and mostly silent when he finds the bag of money, but one can see in his face how poignantly aware he is of the dilemma he has been placed in. He is aware, that is, that taking the money rather than simply leaving it where it lies represents a decision to step outside of his life, to cease being the person he has been. What it means, in fact, is that he will have to become like Chigurh, a person with no fixed location, no firm social attachments, and no stable identity, a kind of stranger in his own land. He does, of course, take the money, and from then on is condemned, as is Chigurh, to an itinerant existence, living alone, sleeping in motels, unable even to rent a car for fear of leaving some trace by which his pursuers might be able to track him.

After injuring each other in a gunfight, both Moss and Chigurh must find ways of treating their injuries that do not involve visiting an American emergency room, where their wounds would surely attract unwanted legal attention. Chigurh arranges to rob a pharmacy so that he can obtain the necessary supplies to perform surgery on himself, which he does in a wince-inducing sequence that reminds us, again, of his beastlike and godlike aspects. Moss, on the other hand, abandons the country altogether, fleeing to Mexico. Before returning he pauses to throw the bag of money, which he cannot declare to the U.S. border monitors, off of the bridge that connects the two countries and into the brush below.

This "no man's land" provides a potent metaphor for the world in which these two characters, in renouncing their ties to their community, have chosen to live. In Mexico, Moss rejects the attempt of bounty hunter Carson Wells to appeal to a shared history of service in Vietnam to establish a bond of kinship:

Wells: Were you in Nam?
Moss: Yeah. I was in Nam.
Wells: So was I.
Moss: So what does that make me? Your buddy?

Ironically, though, Moss discovers that shedding one's loyalties and identities is harder than one might think. On his attempt to return to the U.S.—having lost his ID and nearly all his possessions—the border guard is initially reluctant to readmit him, and it is only his discovery that Moss is a veteran that makes him change his mind. In the border guard's view, the fact that they both served in Vietnam provides the kind of shared bond that mere shared citizenship cannot.

The extent to which Moss has rejected membership in human society is nonetheless clearly established—if by nothing else, then by the fact that he dies both alone and off-screen. The film's center, though, and its moral crux, is neither Moss nor Chigurh but Sheriff Ed Tom Bell. If Chigurh, to borrow Sandel's phrasing, is a paradigm of "a person incapable of constitutive attachments" and hence "a person wholly without character, without moral depth," then Bell is the opposite, the only person in the film who could sincerely say: "I know that I move in a history I neither summon nor command, which carries consequences none the less for my choices and conduct." Indeed, not only is Bell aware of "the moral weight of what he knows," he is nearly overcome by this weight, and spends most the film weighing that burden against the temptation to walk away from his role as a law enforcement officer—a role his father and grandfather before him also occupied—in search of some sort of freedom, some way of being liberated from the bonds, both social and spiritual, that seem to have grown ever more constricting.

As we have observed, loyalty allows for an expansion of one's world: the good of the community to whom one is loyal becomes part of one's own good, and events in the life of one's community become events in one's own life as well. If this is so, then Chigurh represents the limiting case of the person who refuses all such identifications, the person whose life is not embellished or enhanced by any sort of membership or commitment to other human beings. In doing so, he avoids certain costs and dangers we have also noted: the sacrifices our allegiances call on us to make, and the vulnerabilities involved in seeing one's good as united with those of others. Ed Tom Bell, on the other hand, is keenly aware both of what it costs him to belong and of what he would lose in turning away; it is this double awareness that fuels his slow-burning and anguished indecision.

Loyalty is a burden. Whether freely chosen or not, it amounts to a kind of constraint: it limits our individualistic freedom of choice, and it can call on us to make sacrifices, at times significant sacrifices. Moreover, it is easy for an admirable loyalty to slip into one that is anything but; to slide from "I will stand by you no matter what it costs me" to "I will stand by you no matter how badly you treat me" to "I will stand by you no matter how badly you treat others, or how immorally you ask me to behave." We sometimes feel good about being moved by loyalty even when the things it moves us to do are bad—or else, like Ishiguro's Mr. Stevens, we tell ourselves that a clearly wrong action is rendered right by loyalty, and praise ourselves for having the moral fortitude to perform it despite our qualms. As Mary Midgley writes:

> Exploiters and oppressors, war-makers, executioners and destroyers of forests do not usually wear distinctive black hats, nor horns and hooves. The positive motives which move them may not be bad at all; they are often quite decent ones like prudence, loyalty, self-fulfillment and professional conscientiousness. The appalling element lies in the lack of the *other* motives which ought to balance these—in particular, of a proper regard for other people and of a proper priority system which would enforce it.[2]

Loyalty is dangerous because it can make immoral actions—persecuting ethnic minorities, killing in the name of one's country, concealing war crimes committed by one's comrades-in-arms—appear to wear the mantle of virtue. This is how appeals to loyalty convince us to sacrifice ourselves and others. (Tamir describes how the father of a victim of the Hebron massacre told his friends: "Don't come to share your condolences; come to congratulate me. I have become the father of a *shahid*."[3])

But we can also slip out of our loyalties, even out of the best of our loyalties, even without really meaning to. And this possibility also represents a real danger, for though remaining loyal to our communities provides no guarantee that we will avoid moral corruption, since, after all, our communities themselves may be corrupt, neither does turning away from all such claims and living a life unconstrained by loyalties. The truth is that the choice that confronts both Llewellyn Moss and Ed Tom Bell constantly confronts every one of us. We may not pause to dwell on it too often—indeed, we might find it difficult to be sufficiently attentive to our daily lives if we did; but at some level that choice is always present, not only with respect to our countries, but also with respect to our families and friends, and to our principles and causes. Being loyal to anyone or anything is not a matter that can be settled by a single decision, for the option to walk away never ceases to be available. Loyalty changes how we see the world, and so tends to conceal this option, to make it invisible. But it cannot, in doing so, render it unreal.

As tempting as it might be to abandon one's roles and social ties, to try to live a life free from attachments and unhindered by the demands that arise from allegiances, it must not be forgotten that there is an array of goods and of meaningful experiences that is not accessible to the isolated, alienated individual. Along with the capacity for empathy and other moral emotions that Anton Chigurh is lacking, he is also missing something else. There is a realm of meaning and purpose that he seems entirely unable to attain. One suspects, moreover, that he does not even imagine its existence. Loyalty to something larger than oneself, I claimed earlier, makes one's own life larger. It might also be true that one needs to manifest at least a certain degree of loyalty to something other than oneself if one is to have a life at all, in the genuine sense. If my loyalties are among the things that make me the individual I am, then it seems at least possible that a person who had no loyalties would be, quite literally, no one at all.

INTRODUCTION

1 Leslea Newman (2004) *Hachiko Waits*, Henry Holt and Company, New York, NY, p63.

2 John McDowell (1979) "Virtue and reason," *The Monist*, vol 62, pp331–350.

3 Simon Keller makes the interesting suggestion that dogs can be loyal but not disloyal: "You can call a dog loyal, but to call a dog disloyal is to attribute to him motives, and a general level of mental sophistication, that dogs do not possess." Simon Keller (2007) *The Limits of Loyalty*, Cambridge University Press, Cambridge, pp204–205.

4 William Bennett (1993) *The Book of Virtues: A Treasury of Great Moral Stories*, Simon and Schuster, New York, NY, p665.

5 Ann Coulter (2003) *Treason: Liberal Treachery from the Cold War to the War on Terror*, Crown Forum, New York, NY.

6 Jonathan Glover (2000) *Humanity: A Moral History of the Twentieth Century*, Yale University Press, New Haven, CT, pp174–175.

7 Chris Hedges (2010) *Death of the Liberal Class*, Nation Books, New York, NY, pp79–80.

8 Colucci Salutati (1891) *Epistolario di Coluccio Salutati*, F. Novati (ed), Rome, quoted in Maurizio Viroli (1995) *For Love of Country*, Oxford University Press, New York, NY, p27, note 30.

9 Quoted in Glover, *Humanity*, p59.

10 Eric Felten (2011) *Loyalty*, Simon & Schuster, New York, NY, pp66–67.

11 Quoted in Felten, *Loyalty*, p230.

12 Felten, *Loyalty*, p273.

13 I discuss this possibility at greater length in *Love's Vision* (2011) Princeton University Press, Princeton, NJ, especially Chapter 3.

14 See *Love's Vision*.

ONE LOYAL ACTION, LOYAL THOUGHT

1   Yael Tamir (1999) "Pro Patria Mori: Death and State," in M. Steger and
    N. Lind (eds) Violence and Its Alternatives: An Interdisciplinary Reader, Palgrave
    MacMillan, New York, NY, p214.
2   Maurizio Viroli (1995) For Love of Country: An Essay on Patriotism and
    Nationalism, Clarendon Press, Oxford, p32.
3   Morton Grodzins (1956) The Loyal and the Disloyal, University of Chicago
    Press, Chicago, IL, p6.
4   Ernest Partridge (1980) "Why care about the future?," in E. Partridge
    (ed) Responsibilities to Future Generations, Prometheus Books, Buffalo,
    NT, p204.
5   Frederick Exley (1968) A Fan's Notes, Vintage, New York, NY, pp133–134.
6   Frankfurt makes this point in several places; see, for instance, Harry
    G. Frankfurt (2006) Taking Ourselves Seriously and Getting It Right, Stanford
    University Press, Stanford, CA, p25.
7   I do not mean to suggest that what is true of some forms of loyalty—
    that which is properly directed to a baseball team, for instance—
    must be true of all forms. Perhaps patriotism, as a particular form of
    loyalty to country, is unlike baseball team loyalty in that one cannot
    be a patriot without believing one's country to be superior to all other
    countries. My primary point in this paragraph and the three that follow
    is simply to observe that even if this sort of belief is not necessarily
    required, it would be too quick to conclude that no beliefs are required.
8   Philippa Foot makes a similar point about pride in "Moral beliefs":
    Philippa Foot (1978) Virtues and Vices and Other Essays in Moral Philosophy,
    University of California Press, Berkeley, CA.
9   Samuel M. McClure et al (2004) "Neural correlates of behavioral pre-
    ference for culturally familiar drinks," Neuron, vol 44, no 2, 14 October,
    pp379–387.
10 That said, even if you believed the rumors you might defend your
    friend anyway: in at least some cases loyalty does seem to be shown
    by the willingness to defend someone against accusations one knows
    to be true, or to help someone evade the consequences of bad actions
    one acknowledges she has performed. (See the discussion of Andre
    Dubus's "A Father's Story" in Chapter Two.)
11 Simon Keller (2004) "Friendship and belief," Philosophical Papers, vol 33,
    pp329–351, at p333.

12   Sarah Stroud (2006) "Epistemic partiality in friendship," *Ethics*, vol 116, pp498–524, at pp505–506.

13   John McDowell (1998) "The Role of Eudaimonia in Aristotle's ethics," in *Mind, Value, and Reality*, Harvard University Press, Cambridge, MA, p17. See also John McDowell (1979) "Virtue and reason," *The Monist*, vol 62, pp334–335.

14   Kazuo Ishiguro (1989) *The Remains of the Day*, Knopf, New York, NY, pp199–201.

15   Ishiguro, *The Remains of the Day*, p149.

16   Ishiguro, *The Remains of the Day*, p243.

17   Quoted in Eric Felten (2011)

18   Harry Brighouse (2006) *On Education*, Routledge, New York, NY, pp111–112.

19   See Simon Keller (2007)

20   Ishiguro, *The Remains of the Day*, pp147–148.

TWO   CONFLICTS OF LOYALTIES

1   The discussion of the following two paragraphs draws on my paper "Goldstick and the Two-Hats Problem": Troy Jollimore (2003) *Utilitas*, vol 15, no 3, November, pp369–373.

2   André Dubus (1983) "A Father's Story," in *The Times Are Never So Bad*, David R. Godine, Boston, MA.

3   Dubus, "A Father's Story," p175.

4   Dubus, "A Father's Story," p179.

5   Dubus, "A Father's Story," p178.

6   Jean-Paul Sartre (2007) "Existentialism is a humanism," in *Existentialism Is a Humanism*, trans. Carol Macomber, Yale University Press, New Haven, CT, p31.

7   Sartre, "Existentialism is a humanism," p44.

8   Anna Quindlen (2005) *Loud and Clear*, Ballantine, New York, NY, p22.

9   Dubus, "A Father's Story," p172.

10   Jean-Paul Sartre (2007)

11   On incomparability, see the editor's introduction to Ruth Chang (1998) *Incommensurability, Incomparability, and Practical Reason*, Harvard University Press, Boston, MA.

12   Philippa Foot (2002) "Moral realism and moral dilemmas," in *Moral Dilemmas*, Oxford University Press, New York, NY, pp57–58.

THREE LOYALTY, TRIBALISM, VIOLENCE

1   R. Paul Shaw and Yuwa Wong (1989) *Genetic Seeds of Warfare*, Unwin Hyman, London, pp26–27.

2   Gregory Bateson (1977) "From Versailles to cybernetics," in *Steps to an Ecology of Mind*, Ballantine, New York, NY, p470; quoted in Malin Akerstrom (1990) *Betrayal and Betrayers: The Sociology of Treachery*, Transaction Publishers, New Brunswick, NJ, pp1–2.

3   Albert O. Hirschman (1970) *Exit, Voice, and Loyalty: Responses to Decline in Firms, Organizations, and States*, Harvard University Press, Boston, MA.

4   See Alasdair MacIntyre (1981) *After Virtue*, University of Notre Dame Press, Notre Dame, IN; and George Fletcher (1993) *Loyalty: An Essay on the Morality of Relationships*, Oxford University Press, New York/Oxford.

5   Avner de-Shalit (1995) *Why Posterity Matters: Environmental Policies and Future Generations*, Routledge, London, p39.

6   Yael Tamir (1999) "Pro Patria Mori: Death and the state," in M. Steger and N. Lind (eds) *Violence and Its Alternatives: An Interdisciplinary Reader*, Palgrave MacMillan, New York, NY, p215.

7   Tamir, "Pro Patria Mori," p215.

8   Tamir, "Pro Patria Mori," p214.

9   Quoted in James McPherson (1997) *For Cause and Comrades: Why Men Fought in the Civil War*, Oxford University Press, New York, NY, p98.

10 Benedict Anderson (1983) *Imagined Communities*, Verso, London.

11 George Kateb (2006) "Is patriotism a mistake?," in *Patriotism and Other Mistakes*, Yale University Press, New Haven, CT, pp3–20, p8.

12 Chris Hedges (2000) "What I read at war", *Harvard Magazine*, July–August.

13 Josiah Royce (1995, originally published 1908) *The Philosophy of Loyalty*, Vanderbilt University Press, Nashville, TN, p8.

14 *The Collected Poems of Rupert Brooke* (1919) Dodd, Mead & Co., New York, NY, p115.

15 Wilfred Owen (1920) *Poems*, Chatto & Windus, London, p15.

16 Randall Jarrell (1969) *The Complete Poems*, Farrar, Straus, and Giroux, New York, NY, p144.

17 Jonathan Glover (1999)

18 Quoted in Peter L. Berger (1972) "Languages of murder," *World View*, vol 15, p10.

19 U.S. Army (2003) *The Soldier's Guide*, October, http://www.smdc.army.
mil/2008/CSM/docs/FM7_21_13.pdf, Section 1–3, accessed 25
August 2011.

20 Kateb, "Is patriotism a mistake?", p9.

FOUR LOYALTY, COMMUNITY, AND MORALITY

1 Royce, *The Philosophy of Loyalty*, p. 47.

2 Andrew Oldenquist (2002) "Loyalties," in I. Primoratz (ed) *Patriotism*,
Humanity Books, Amherst, NY, p31.

3 Alasdair MacIntyre (1994) "Is patriotism a virtue?", in M. Daly (ed)
Communitarianism: A New Public Ethics, Wadsworth Publishing Company,
Belmont, CA, pp307–318, at p312.

4 Michael Sandel (1998) *Liberalism and the Limits of Justice*, Cambridge
University Press, Boston, MA, p179.

5 Michael Ondaatje (1992) *The English Patient: A Novel*, Knopf, New York,
NY, p14. Further references to this novel are given parenthetically
in the text.

6 That we are is further reinforced by the story of Kip, the Indian sapper
who spends the war risking his life to defuse bombs for the British
only to end up feeling shocked and exploited when the Allies drop two
nuclear bombs on Japan. The bombing renders him unable to continue
his romance with Hana, and leads him to rediscover his identity as
a non-English citizen, if not as an Indian. The novel leaves it open
whether Kip's rebellion is against universal morality itself (whether,
that is, he becomes a kind of communitarian at the end of the book),
or against the claims of the British and American empires to embody
that universal morality.

7 Representative thinkers might include Kwame A. Appiah (2006)
Cosmopolitanism: Ethics in a World of Strangers, W. W. Norton, New York, NY;
Simon Caney (2005) *Justice Beyond Borders: A Global Political Theory*, Oxford
University Press, Oxford; David Held (2005) *Cosmopolitanism: A Defense*,
Polity Press, New York, NY; and Martha Nussbaum (2002) "Patriotism
and cosmopolitanism," in M. Nussbaum and J. Cohen (eds) *For Love of
Country?*, Beacon Press, Boston, MA.

8 The level of self-involvement seems to be greater in Anthony
Minghella's 1996 film version of the novel, which has Almásy
explaining his decision to return to Katherine at all costs by saying:

"I had to get back to the desert. I'd made a promise. *The rest meant nothing to me* [emphasis inserted]."

9   MacIntyre, "Is patriotism a virtue?", pp307–318, at p312.
10   Sandel, *Liberalism and the Limits of Justice*, p180.
11   Anna Stilz (2009) *Liberal Loyalty*, Princeton University Press, Princeton, NJ, p18.
12   See especially Peter Singer (2000) *Writings on an Ethical Life*, Ecco, New York, NY.
13   Jean-Paul Sartre (2007)

CONCLUSION

1   Aristotle, *Politics*, 1253a.
2   Mary Midgley (1984, reprinted 1996) *Wickedness: A Philosophical Essay*, Routledge, New York, NY, p67.
3   Yael Tamir (1999)